PRAISE FOR
EVERYTHING HIDDEN
SHALL BE REVEALED

"Not since reading John L. McKenzie's *Authority in the Church* have I found myself so moved to challenge the quotidian assumptions regarding episcopal authority that have so easily worked their way into my own ministry. The sexual abuse crisis in the Church today is in many ways the result of the religiously-endorsed exercise of dominative power. The present work cannot be overlooked without the risk of perpetuating the same dynamic.

We need not agree with every one of DeVille's analyses or prescriptions—and I do not—to find in this book a roadmap toward recovery. His vision is at once forward-thinking and eminently traditional. Without a doubt this is a book that can raise quite a stir. And I hope it will. It deserves serious, prayerful reading."

—**MOST REV. JOHN MICHAEL BOTEAN**, Romanian Catholic Bishop of Canton, OH

"In this provocative and serious book, Adam DeVille presents radical ways of transforming the Church through a return to synodal and conciliar structures rooted in the traditions of the ancient Church. If there is to be death and resurrection for the Church, a Paschal renewal, then this must be the return of the Church to what it is: the assembly, not just in principle but in practice, of the *whole people* of God. His is a strong, courageous challenge to an embattled and damaged Church."

—**THE V. REV. MICHAEL PLEKON**, Professor Emeritus, City University of New York

"This book eloquently and cogently pleads for the Roman Catholic Church to be released from the captivity of an over-centralized, over-individualized model of authority, arguing that this model is at the heart of many other dysfunctionalities. While we should harbor no illusions about the problems alternative systems may face, Adam DeVille makes a strong case for seeing the existing paradigm as both quite recent in its development and as consolidating a damaging set of attitudes to clerical power. A sober, theologically informed, and very significant work."

— RT. REV. ROWAN WILLIAMS, Master of Magdalene College, University of Cambridge

"Searing and fearless, Adam DeVille humanizes the meaning of the sexual abuse crisis in the Catholic Church and calls for a radical reconfiguration of the exercise of power. The demythologizing of clerics is beyond urgent, as is the rejection of church-distorting papal idolatry—both requiring retrieval of the best models of the Christian East, where the conciliar nature of the Orthodox and Eastern Catholic traditions has long recognized that authoritarian clerical oversight is a threat to the fundamental nature of the Church. Professor DeVille's vision will frighten many a hierarch, because only a Church in which bishops, clergy, and laity share authority (in equal-but-different relationships) can rescue Catholicism from cultural and spiritual shipwreck."

— RT. REV. ARCHPRIEST LAWRENCE CROSS, St. Kilda East, Melbourne, Australia

"In *Everything Hidden Shall Be Revealed*, Adam DeVille has written a book with something for everybody to hate and something to incline everybody (or almost everybody) to nod and say, 'Yes, that's exactly right.' Either way, readers with open minds and generous hearts will find this a provocative, helpful contribution to the badly needed debate about reform in the Church at a moment when reform is so urgently needed."

— RUSSELL SHAW, former Secretary for Public Affairs of the National Conference of Catholic Bishops/United States Catholic Conference; author of *Nothing to Hide: Secrecy, Communication, and Communion in the Catholic Church*

"Adam DeVille begins his book with the jolting pronouncement that 'everything hidden must be revealed' regarding the present sex-abuse crisis in the Catholic Church. But this is only the first step. Writing with exceptional passion, he turns next, in an unexpected (but welcome) way, to a serious consideration of Orthodox ecclesiology and existing Orthodox ecclesiastical arrangements in order to identify a path that might allow Roman Catholics to move past 'the current papal-centric structure' and toward a Church in which authority and decision-making power is more jointly shared by laity, clergy, and bishops. Orthodox may benefit from DeVille's studied perspective on their own churches, which well illustrates how renewal and reform might be accomplished for them as well."

— **VIGEN GUROIAN**, Armenian Orthodox theologian, author of *The Orthodox Reality: Culture, Theology, and Ethics in the Modern World*

"Adam DeVille continues the line of great Catholic theologians who have asked uncomfortable questions and provided unconventional solutions to ecclesiological issues. DeVille takes the baton from the hands of Congar, Rahner, Murray, and Küng, in serving the Church with both *aggiornamento* and *ressourcement*. But the true source of his inspiration is Eastern Christianity, in its Greek Catholic, Byzantine, and Oriental Orthodox forms, which provide serious challenges to the modern ways of exercising primacy and synodality in the Roman Catholic Church. Without this book, any serious ecumenical discussion between Westerners and Easterners on the church-dividing issues would be incomplete."

— **ARCHIMANDRITE CYRIL HOVORUN**, director of the Huffington Ecumenical Institute, Loyola Marymount University, Los Angeles, CA

"In this timely, courageous, and, certainly, controversial book, theologian Adam DeVille examines the current (and seemingly perpetual) crisis in the Church and the culture and assumptions that allowed it to take root and flourish. Deploying exceptional knowledge of Church history and awareness of ecclesial structures both inside and outside the Catholic Church, DeVille deconstructs the ruling idols of the Catholic imaginary and cuts to the core of the rampant pathologies haunting the ecclesial psyche. Along the way he exposes the all-too-often warped and anachronistic practices that have contributed to Catholicism's current predicament. Turning to Freud, DeVille follows the import of Christ's directive to 'call no man father' (Matt. 23:9), then offers alternative structures that would steady the bark of the Church, broaching even the possibility not only of a married priesthood, but of married bishops. In *Everything Hidden Shall Be Revealed*, Adam DeVille summons the necessary courage to face this fateful moment with brutal honesty, but not without hope."

— **MICHAEL MARTIN**, author of *Transfiguration: Notes Toward a Radical Catholic Reimagination of Everything*

"Adam DeVille's proposal for cleansing and reform in the Catholic Church today is crystal-clear: the Church must stop *being governed* by a caste of clerical guardians and start *governing itself.* How might this happen? The way it has always happened: through the practice of conciliar government, or to speak Greek, synodal government. Councils are not a panacea against mortal ills, but they do excel over all the alternatives when it comes to the cardinal virtue of a system of government — namely, accountability. Conciliar government is shared government. DeVille wants to see it instituted on all levels: parish, diocese, national church, and global communion. In this learned, passionate, and ecumenically informed book, DeVille leaves his readers eager to get to work on his proposal *today.*"

— **PAUL VALLIERE**, Professor Emeritus, Butler University, author of *Modern Russian Theology* and *Conciliarism*

"In this fascinating volume that builds upon his previous books on the papacy and on married priesthood, DeVille makes a compelling argument that in its current crisis the Catholic Church requires nothing less than the death of old structures, with new ones emerging in their place. The Catholic Church needs to abandon papal-episcopal monopoly on power and embrace traditional (and time-tested) joint forms of governing involving both laity and clergy. His pragmatic proposals would make it harder to commit and hide abuses at parish, diocesan, national, and universal levels; and he concludes with a defence of married priests and bishops. DeVille's painfully honest analysis, informed with his long-established academic rigor, creativity, and captivating style, makes for gripping reading wedded to an implementable call to action."

— **RADU BORDEIANU**, Associate Professor of Theology, Duquesne University

"Intelligent and provocative, this book is written out of a deep love for the Church. One needn't agree with DeVille on every point to profit from his perceptive analysis of the present ecclesial situation and from his proposals for reform."

— **CHRISTOPHER J. RUDDY**, Associate Professor of Systematic Theology, Catholic University of America

Everything Hidden
Shall Be Revealed

Everything Hidden Shall Be Revealed

Ridding the Church of Abuses of Sex and Power

ADAM A. J. DEVILLE

Angelico Press

For information, address:
Angelico Press, Ltd.
169 Monitor St.
Brooklyn, NY 11222
www.angelicopress.com

pb 978-1-62138-437-3
cloth 978-1-62138-438-0
ebook 978-1-62138-439-7

Book and cover design
by Michael Schrauzer

Contents

Introduction

A DECADE AGO I FINISHED A RATHER CON-
servative and scholarly treatment of the papacy and its role
in advancing Christian unity, especially with the Orthodox
East.[1] Little could I imagine then how much of what I wrote would
remain even more relevant today in light of the relentless news about
hierarchical malfeasance and malevolence in committing and covering up sexual abuse in Australia, Argentina, Ireland, India, Germany,
Canada, Honduras, and across these United States. Little could I have
known that my thoughts ten years ago would now seem too narrow, and
that what is required are more radical reforms than what I proposed
in *Orthodoxy and the Roman Papacy*. But here we are.

The crisis of today is not just of sex abuse but also the abuse of
power, and both of these have been able to hide behind current church
structures for far too long. If we are ever to see the end of this crisis,
then everything hidden must, first, be revealed. That is a preliminary
step that everyone agrees upon. But, second, the hiding places must be
abolished before, third, new structures are re-created to take the place
of the old ones, allowing for openness in decision-making and mutual
accountability between all three orders within the Church—hierarchs,
clerics, and laics.

These latter two steps have not been carefully thought through until
now. This book does exactly that, making arguments for why the old
structures must be abolished, and why new ones (which are actually
very ancient, and much more justified by both history and theology)
installed in their place. Such a call for abolition is revolutionary in
nature, for it is only with and after the revolution that the Church will
ever experience true resurrection. Until and unless there is a death to
the old self-conceptions of the Church and its old ways of structuring its
life, the possibility of the Church emerging from the tomb into newer

---

1 *Orthodoxy and the Roman Papacy: Ut Unum Sint and the Prospects of East-West
Unity* (University of Notre Dame Press, 2011).

and purer life is foreclosed. All the old, romanticized pious platitudes about simply fasting and praying more, or waiting for better popes and bishops, are now revealed to be not just ineffective but positively destructive. Tinkering will not save us.

I should say at the outset what this book is not: it is not a first-aid manual to stop the hemorrhaging happening right now. I have elsewhere put forward ideas to staunch the blood flow in the present. This book instead looks to the long-term, knowing that the Church has always been in it for the long haul. The changes proposed here will take some time to bring about, and will thereafter require long-term commitments for their on-going implementation in a much differently structured and governed Church.

I should also stress that the ideas in this book are not the product of haste or of panic. These ideas are not forms of jerry-rigged ecclesiastical engineering trying to stave off a flood in progress. Rather, almost all the things I argued here have been proposed before over the past dozen and more years in a variety of journals, public lectures, published chapters in books, and other fora. They are based on serious and solid historical and ecclesiological scholarship of the last several decades. This book brings all that together and revises what I have learned in the intervening years to present a fresh analysis of major reforms in a structured and systematic way.

I should also add, and will here stress, that even if this sex abuse crisis went away tomorrow, I would defend the reforms proposed here for the same four reasons that have led me to write this book in the first place: their history, their ecumenical appeal, their practical benefits, and above all their theology. Of these four, this book primarily addresses the third—the practical benefits of renewed structures at the parochial, diocesan and national levels as ways of addressing the sex-abuse crisis. But it does so because of the fourth—the theological argumentation supporting my proposed reforms. Along the way, their historical supports are noted while their ecumenical appeal is clear but not treated directly.

But the theological case for these reforms is adamantine. To state it baldly at the outset: the vision fleshed out here of the Church as governed jointly by the laics, the clergy, and the bishops, is far more theologically justifiable and defensible than the current papal-centric structure with its papal-episcopal monopoly on power. That monopolistic structure is a huge problem in itself, contributing in significant measure to the current crisis. It is also theologically perverse and lacking coherent theological justification. It must go.

If my previous book was focused on high-level reforms to the papacy at the upper reaches of the Church, with an eye to ecumenical outreach towards the Orthodox, the reforms proposed in this book are all heavily focused on the local and the regional structures of the Church — or, rather, the lack thereof. It is their lack that is the real problem in this crisis, and the return of these structures in their fullest form (for many already exist in part, often under unjustifiable restrictions) will be a major part of the recovery.

Ecclesiological Excursus

MY FOCUS IN THIS BOOK IS ON, PRIMARILY, THE LATIN Church, more popularly known as the Roman Catholic Church. The Latin Church is the largest (having over 1 billion members) of the global Catholic communion of churches, which includes twenty-three other Catholic churches known collectively as the Eastern ("Oriental") Catholic Churches. These are comparatively small in aggregate (c. 20 million faithful) and have very distinctive and obvious liturgical customs, architecture, and iconography, all of which are visible any time you enter, say, a Ukrainian Catholic or Armenian Catholic or Coptic Catholic or Melkite Catholic church building. Less obvious are their ancient structures and practices which I shall draw on in this book, including the ideas of local election of bishops, synodal governance in dioceses and regions, and the possibility of both a married priesthood and episcopate. All these churches are in communion with the Latin or West-Roman[2] Church and her universal head, the bishop of Rome.[3]

---

2 So called because those we have, since Gibbon, termed "Byzantines" saw themselves as East Romans, that is citizens of the Roman Empire in the east, which lasted long after it had collapsed in the West.

3 Short, accessible and reliable overviews are to be found in Joan L. Roccasalvo, *The Eastern Catholic Churches: An Introduction to Their Worship and Spirituality* (Liturgical

They are equally Catholic, but Catholic here has never meant, and must never be taken to mean, a homogenous set of exclusively Latin or West-Roman practices. To use a not entirely satisfactory, but nonetheless common, metaphor, the Church has two lungs—the West, but also the East. Neither lung can lay claim to being more Catholic than the other; neither is more important.

This book, then, is written by a Catholic who is not a Latin, and it proposes several structures found at least partially in other Catholic churches — except, peculiarly, the Latin or Roman Catholic Church. (There is no coherent *theological* reason why these structures might be good and permissible in one or more Eastern Catholic churches but somehow forbidden to the Latin Church.) The perspective here, then, is what one might call an "outsider's *inside* perspective."[4] I am outside the particular Latin Church, but inside the universal Catholic Church. Why, then, do I feel that I should address these concerns to the Latin Church?

There are, at risk of sounding pious, two words in answer to that question: love and communion: I am in communion with the Latin Church, and I love her. And love means bearing with her sufferings, and, even more, trying to find ways to alleviate them.

But rather than listen to me explain how it is that I can presume to write the things I shall in this book, listen instead to the far greater

---

Press, 1992); Edward Faulk, *101 Questions and Answers on Eastern Catholic Churches* (Paulist Press, 2007); and Fred Saato, *American Eastern Catholics* (Paulist, 2006). For those who want a more scholarly resource with a lot of hard data (membership statistics, addresses to contact bishops, etc.) then see Ronald Roberson's utterly invaluable *The Eastern Churches: A Brief Survey*, 7th ed. (Pontifical Oriental Institute Press, 2005). This book covers all the Orthodox as well as Eastern Catholic churches.

4 If some autobiography may intrude here for a moment, I would note that I am a faithful son of the Catholic Church, and I teach at a Catholic university where I hold a *mandatum* from the local Latin bishop. In essence, this is what, in other professions and disciplines, might be called a license to practice — as teachers and clinicians hold — saying I have been trained and committed myself to doing what the licensing body — the local church in this case in the person of her bishop — requires of me faithfully to do. As an Eastern Catholic cleric with my own bishop, seeking this was not required of me, for the bishop of Ft. Wayne–South Bend is not my ordinary (cf. CCEO c. 327). I asked for the *mandatum* to demonstrate my desire and commitment always to teach in full communion with the Church and never to teach any doctrine contrary to revealed and defined teachings.

eloquence of the apostle to the nations writing to the Corinthians:

> Now there are varieties of gifts, but the same Spirit; and there
> are varieties of service, but the same Lord; and there are vari-
> eties of working, but it is the same God who inspires them all
> in every one. To each is given the manifestation of the Spirit
> for the common good. (I Cor. 12:4–7)

I would ask readers, above all Latin Catholics, to receive what is written
here as a gift offered in service to the Spirit for the common good of all
Catholics throughout the world. I write for no other purpose than that.

The structural reforms proposed here have the benefit of being tried
and tested previously in many places in the wider Christian world. St.
Paul finishes his metaphor and reflection with this:

> On the contrary, the parts of the body which seem to be
> weaker are indispensable, and those parts of the body which
> we think less honorable we invest with the greater honor, and
> our unpresentable parts are treated with greater modesty,
> which our more presentable parts do not require. But God
> has so composed the body, giving the greater honor to the
> inferior part, that there may be no discord in the body, but
> that the members may have the same care for one another.
> (I Cor. 12:22–25)

In this moment of supreme crisis for the Latin Church — but really for
the entire Catholic Church — it behooves Eastern Christians not to stand
around doing nothing, but to offer possible gifts and indispensable
practices from their own rich patrimony. In doing so, we are offering
proof of the "same care for one another" that Paul commands us to have.

As I am offering these ideas as gifts, I keep before my mind's eye
the weaknesses of my own Ukrainian Greco-Catholic Church[5] — and,
indeed, all the Eastern Churches, Catholic and Orthodox. There is none

---

5 In which — in the interests of full disclosure — I am a cleric in minor orders as
an ordained subdeacon.

perfect among us except Christ. None, therefore, has the right to crow of their own superiority, or to say to others "I have no need of you." As a scholar of the Christian East and severe critic of any attempts at romanticizing or idealizing the historical record of the Church (East or West), I have long resisted the silly on-line (and sometimes printed) tracts by apologists who slander and misrepresent the West to make the East look good: every fault of the former — no matter how slight or even imaginary — is trotted out as a foil to make the latter's supposed virtues gleam all the brighter. You will find no such nonsense here.

For, in fact, the East, especially but not exclusively among Eastern Catholics, has only imperfectly realized several of the practices I shall sketch out here. For too long too much of Eastern Catholic reality was governed by an inferiority complex in which what was distinctive about the East was downplayed or abandoned so as to adopt supposedly superior Latin practices. To give the most germane example: synodal elections of bishops is still only partially realized in the Eastern Catholic world, as it, too, has felt the massive pressures of the papal machine's desire to dominate everything in its path. Thus, Eastern Catholics have *sometimes* elected *some* of their bishops but only in *some* parts of the world. The East, then, has no grounds for feeling smug or superior here. And, in fact, what I write — largely directed to the Latin Church because that is where most of the crisis is to be found today — needs to be applied more widely across *all* the Eastern Catholic Churches, too. These proposals, then, apply to *all* the Catholic churches of East *and* West to the extent that they have not fulfilled them completely. The East has a bit of a head-start. That is all.

But do not make the mistake of assuming that what I am proposing here is *exclusively* of Eastern provenance. As I shall show, much of what is proposed here was at one time found in the Latin Church throughout the West, but fell into disuse — sometimes slowly, and sometimes with a great big, and often politically motivated, shove. Moreover, some of these practices exist even today within other parts of the Western Christian tradition, including the Anglican Communion. These are gifts offered from the East and from Anglicanism only because the West has forgotten that it, too, once had them. Thus these proposals cannot be dismissed by calling them "Protestantizing" or, still less, "Easternizing" or "Byzantinizing." They are, quite simply, Catholic — even if they have been forgotten[6] by most Catholics. They exist within Catholic tradition and long-term historical memory.

Receiving Gifts from History and from Other Christians

THE IDEA OF RETRIEVING GIFTS IS MADE ABUNDANTLY clear in the excellent new document of the International Theological Commission (ITC) where it rightly argues that synodal governance

> offers a specific description of the historical development of the Church as such [and] breathes life into her structures and directs her mission. The Trinitarian, anthropological, Christological, pneumatological and Eucharistic dimensions of God's plan of salvation, which is at work in the mystery of the Church, are the theological horizon which has been the context for the development of synodality across the centuries.[7]

I draw on examples deeply rooted "across the centuries" in Catholic and Christian tradition, East and West, of the first millennium and much of the second, because everything that is good in the wider tradition is part of the genuine catholicity of the Church and part of her living and authentically universal tradition. We must be clear here that "Catholic tradition" as I shall use it (i) goes all the way back to the beginning of the Church at the hands of Christ on earth; (ii) includes the entire Christian East; and (iii) is the Church's memory where we may legitimately find and restore to renewed use what has been temporarily forgotten or set aside, often for no clear reason, in the understanding that all of it is genuinely of God, even if its practice

6 See Francis Oakley's *The Conciliarist Tradition: Constitutionalism in the Catholic Church 1300–1870* (Oxford University Press, 2008) for how much was deliberately forgotten — indeed, suppressed — after the Council of Constance; and see Joseph Mueller's detailed typology of examples in "Forgetting as a Principle of Continuity in Tradition," *Theological Studies* 70 (2009): 751–81.

7 ITC, "Synodality in the Life and Mission of the Church Today," no. 48: http://www.vatican.va/roman_curia/congregations/cfaith/cti_documents/rc_cti _20180302_sinodalita_en.html.

has not been widely seen in contemporary Roman Catholic practice. Tradition is thus seen expansively, historically, and ecumenically, as indeed it only can be. The truly Catholic mind does not disdain what *appears* to be extraneous but seeks to "test everything" and to "hold fast what is good" wherever it may be found (I Thess. 5:21).

In other words, the fact that some of what I describe currently resides in or is practiced by other Christians — the Armenian Orthodox above all — should not trouble Catholics at all. If it is good, beautiful, and true, and if it contributes to the upbuilding of the Body of Christ, then its provenance is very nearly irrelevant. Roman Catholics are invited to see the good practices of other Christians and to think about incorporating them into their own church now in her moment of grave peril. For this is the teaching of the Catholic Church at the Second Vatican Council:

> Moreover, some and even very many of the significant elements and endowments which together go to build up and give life to the Church itself can exist outside the visible boundaries of the Catholic Church: the written word of God; the life of grace; faith, hope and charity, with the other interior gifts of the Holy Spirit, and visible elements too. All of these, which come from Christ and lead back to Christ, belong by right to the one Church of Christ. (*Unitatis Redintegratio* no. 3)

In bringing out these proposals from the wider tradition and historical patrimony of the Church, I am further following the example of Vatican II, which argued that part of the divine constitution of the Church is precisely her ongoing call to reform:

> Christ summons the Church to continual reformation as she sojourns here on earth. The Church is always in need of this, in so far as she is an institution of men here on earth. Thus if, in various times and circumstances, there have been deficiencies in moral conduct or in church discipline, . . . these can and should be set right at the opportune moment. (*Unitatis Redintegratio* no. 6)

Now is the opportune time, more than ever, to begin this work of "continual reformation," a process in which I am guided by the Council's greatest theologian, Yves Congar, who, in his 1950 book *Vraie et fausse réforme dans l'Eglise,* argued that "the great law of Catholic reform begins with a return to the principles of Catholicism. It is necessary to interrogate the tradition and to dive back into it, understanding that 'tradition' does not mean 'routine' nor even, properly, 'the past.'"[8]

In bringing these proposals forward from the past or from the present life of other churches today, we are inspired and guided by the model of the late Pope John Paul II, who often wrote and spoke of an "ecumenical gift exchange."[9] That notion of an ecumenical gift exchange was given striking new articulation in the summer of 2018 with the release of a document from the Anglican-Roman Catholic International Commission (ARCIC) entitled "Walking Together on the Way: Learning to Be the Church — Local, Regional, Universal." This document calls upon Catholics "to look humbly at what is not working effectively *within one's own tradition,* and . . . to ask whether this might be helped by receptive learning from the understanding, structures, practices, and judgements of the other" (no. 78; their emphasis). As I will show — particularly in the chapter on diocesan synods — the structures and practices of Anglicanism have a lot to offer the contemporary Catholic Church.

To a certain type of Catholic, that claim may cause great unease: Anglicans have something to offer Catholics? Isn't Anglicanism falling apart with its gay priests, lesbian bishops, and numberless innovations? Here I ask Roman Catholics to receive these proposals precisely as gift, and to do so without smugness or skepticism. Smugness, as Flannery O'Connor once said, is the besetting Catholic sin: the temptation is to assume that the Catholic Church is the perfect church and her "divine constitution" has no need of change.

I am well aware of the disarray within Anglicanism, having been part of that communion for a quarter-century. But Catholics must

---

8 This is my translation from the French original (pp. 335–36), which I read many years before the new English translation emerged.

9 See his thoughts on this in a variety of places, including his 1995 encyclical *Ut Unum Sint.*

be prone to an acute form of sanctimonious blindness to assume that there is no such disarray within Catholicism. To those worried that some of my proposals, especially for synods, may bring about within Catholicism similar divisions as those within Anglicanism, I would ask them to think on several things. First, unlike Anglicanism, the Catholic Church has a defined magisterial function, which it has not been shy about exercising on critical doctrinal matters (none of which are disputed here by me in any way). Second, even exercising that authority has not quelled a lot of open and covert dissent within the Catholic Church. Nevertheless, there *is* an entire body of authoritative teaching on questions of both faith and morals — ranging from the nature of the Eucharist to artificial insemination — that Anglicanism simply lacks. These will not change, and one does not have to guess what the Church teaches. To put it bluntly, Catholicism has the capacity to produce, and has produced, an authoritative universal catechism; Anglicanism has neither. I fully support and believe all that the Catholic Church teaches, and nothing proposed here seeks to do anything otherwise. That body of teaching is not going away, and its status cannot be undone by popular vote.

A related concern must also be put to rest: provincial autonomy (as Anglicans call it), or what in the Orthodox East is referred to as autocephaly. What is proposed here is not to recreate those systems (which have significant problems, not least nationalism, of which I am an enemy).[10] What is proposed here are modified versions whereby what is best in provincial and regional structures is maintained while also accounting for a significant role exercised by the bishop of Rome as the universal "sentinel" whose job "consists precisely in 'keeping watch' (episkopein)" over "all the particular Churches" in which "the una, sancta, catholica et apostolica Ecclesia is made present" as Pope John Paul II put it so compellingly.[11]

---

10   In this regard, see the splendid essay of John O'Malley, "Vatican I: Loss and Gain in the Catholic Church," *Church Life Journal,* November 5, 2018, http://churchlife. nd.edu/2018/11/05/vatican-i-loss-and-gain-in-the-governance-of-the-catholic-church/.

11   *Ut Unum Sint* no. 94.

Ecclesiastical Structures: What Is Possible?

MY PROPOSALS, THEN, ARE IN THE REALM OF ECCLESIOL-
ogy generally (and not, say, moral theology or Christology), and ecclesial
structures more particularly. To use a well-known distinction, I am
proposing changes to discipline, not doctrine; to pastoral practices and
processes, not to dogmatic truths. There is, of course, a close connection
between the two—or there should be—and, in fact, what I propose
here will help the doctrine of God to shine more brightly through the
structures of a repristinated Church that will more luminously be an
icon of the Trinity. Thus the Church must change, as Cyril Hovorun
has recently put it, "in order to correspond more truly in its human
and historical dimension to what God wants it to be."[12]

Ecclesiology is the realm of theology much more flexible and
malleable in nature than others, for it concerns, above all, human
structures used by human beings in the Church on earth to meet
current exigencies. The problem comes in mistaking those structures
as somehow being more permanent, more important, more immobile,
and more than human — almost or indeed fully divine, or at least of
divine origin. But they are not. Ecclesial structures, in Cyril Hovorun's
helpful recent imagery, should be understood as scaffolding, and
scaffolding, as we know, is temporary and teleological: it acts towards
some greater end or good. Scaffolding exists not for its own sake but
to support and bolster another in pursuit of its goals. It is designed
to be moved around as tasks demand. It is, then, entirely natural that
such alterations and reconfigurations as proposed here will allow the
Church to emerge, on the far side of my "construction site," much purer
and stronger, and more able to show to the world her inner nature as
"a sacrament or as a sign and instrument both of a very closely knit
union with God and of the unity of the whole human race" (*Lumen
Gentium* no. 1). As Hovorun has put it, such "work of deconstruction
does not seek to destroy the structures but rather to keep them open

---

12 Cyril Hovorun, *Scaffolds of the Church: Towards Post-Structural Ecclesiology*
(Cascade, 2017), 12. Interestingly, in this passage Hovorun—who is Orthodox—is
summarizing what a lot of contemporary Roman Catholic ecclesiologists have said
about the necessity of change.

so they can be readjusted to their original meaning,"[13] which is, of course, communion with God.

These reforms, to be sure, are far-reaching, but the times demand them. That should be clear to everyone living through this time of crisis. What is equally if not more clear is that pious exhortations to pray and fast *unless accompanied by major structural reforms* are totally insufficient to the task at hand. Indeed, following one of my major interlocutors in this book — the Spanish Jesuit theologian and psychoanalyst Carlos Dominguez-Morano — I would go so far as to say, as he recently has, that exhortations from hierarchs to the faithful to pray and fast more can mask a sinister agenda on behalf of the former against the latter: "religious power structures have never been indifferent to prayer and have so frequently manipulated it to their advantage.... Prayer finds in power a perfect ally and associate to help pursue certain goals, not always clear in their evangelical motivations." Those goals, I would suggest, usually include the unspoken domination and enforced silence of the people instructed to pray, for such praying, it is confidently assumed, will be not to ask God to "scatter the proud in the imagination of their hearts" and to "put down the mighty from their [episcopal] thrones" (Luke 1:51–52). Rather, the praying one is told to do is little more than a diversionary tactic designed to avoid conflict and any serious demands for real change on the part of those in power:

> On these occasions when the subject finds himself in conflict and in disagreement with certain approaches from authority, it is frightening to hear that old "pray on it" advice. Frightening because we are left doubting whether what is really wanted is that the matter is taken up with the God of Jesus of Nazareth or with the god of that figure in the unconscious, the superego.[14]

The problem with praying to an image of a god projected by our superego onto the living God is that our "superego makes us incredibly

---

13 Ibid., 181.

14 Carlos Dominguez-Morano, *Belief after Freud: Religious Faith through the Crucible of Psychoanalysis*, trans. F. J. Montero (Routledge, 2018), 94–95.

obedient."[15] The image of God in our superego is "the father image in whose face the only option is submission to the law."[16] This is the God popes and bishops want us to pray to, but it is an illusion and a neurotic idol from which we must be freed, as I shall argue in my first chapter.

It is clear by now that idolatry, especially of the papacy but to a lesser extent surrounding bishops and other clergy in the Church, has played an enormous, but hitherto undiagnosed, part in the present crisis. Only very slowly are some Catholics even beginning to question, let alone shed, their lingering illusions about their popes, bishops, and priests, realizing that we can no longer assume *prima facie* their trustworthiness, never mind holiness.

Never again can we assume that abusers are either "conservative" or "liberal," progressives or traditionalists. They come from every part of the Church, and so every part of the Church must change. Out of the ruins of an unjustifiable system we will find the possibility of rebuilding along very different lines. This is a task we cannot shirk if we are ever to climb out of this cesspool and prevent further falls into future pools. To prevent that unhappy fate from occurring again, we must move now to put into place structures that will prevent unaccountable bishops from doing as they please.

This is not, let it be noted, "clericalizing the laity" as some would claim in trying to deflect attention from the kinds of necessary reforms proposed here. It is unfolding the theology proclaimed by the Church from her foundations, a theology recently and succinctly described by the International Theological Commission as the "synodal calling of the people of God" based on their indelible "baptismal dignity" which manifests itself in the "co-responsibility of all." For the Church properly understood and structured, "the participation of the lay faithful becomes essential."[17] Following this impeccable theology, then, what I propose is *not* for the laics to take over and muscle aside clerics and bishops, but to move into their rightful role long since denied them by modern

---

15 Ibid.
16 Ibid.
17 ITC, "Synodality in the Life and Mission of the Church Today," no. 72, http://www.vatican.va/roman_curia/congregations/cfaith/cti_documents/rc_cti_20180302_sinodalita_en.html.

canons and practices that are neither historically nor theologically justifiable — as the ITC admits. Nothing proposed here would have laics attempting to celebrate the Eucharist or perform ordinations, or to issue new (or alter past) decrees on doctrine. Rather, the proposals bring them into the structures of governance of the Church, which are currently perverted by the absence of the laics and thus prone to the perverse abuses we are seeing. The proposals, in short, are guided by one crucial principle: *nobody in any context for any reason at any point in human history deserves to have a monopoly on power of any sort.*

It must be noted here, however, that no structures are fail-safe; no systems or processes are perfect; none can perfectly guarantee there will be no future problems. The structures and systems proposed here will bring their own challenges with them, which must be faced honestly, and by all concerned. For all systems and structures must be planned and executed by flawed and fallible human beings, and they are therefore prone to abuse and misuse because of the effects of original sin and human weakness.[18]

Nevertheless, precisely to guard as much as possible against the effects of sinfulness and selfishness, these proposals aim to be durable and difficult to circumvent, making it much harder to perpetrate abuses in the first place and to perpetuate them by covering them up. Everything proposed here has those twin goals: to make it harder to commit, and harder to hide. We will do this by developing open lines of mutual deference and accountability — rather than isolating bishops and having them be accountable to nobody, at least in practice. For such systems always — *always* — end in nothing but disaster. Such systems seek not the propagation of the gospel, but the propagation of themselves and their own power. They are what Avery Dulles denounced as "institutionalism . . . , a system in which the institutional element

---

18 For this reason, I am nowhere suggesting that the structures proposed here must be adopted in exactly the same form by all Catholics everywhere and for all time. Ecclesial structures must remain provisional and teleological. I fully expect that, even if these proposals were implemented, in time the Church would continue to make adjustments, and this is entirely fitting and appropriate. Mine are not eternal verities carved in stone, but arguments for practices needed *right now*. Future generations may well find the need for different practices to deal with different problems in their own time.

is treated as primary.... Institutionalism is a deformation of the true nature of the Church — a deformation that has unfortunately affected the Church . . . and remains in every age a real danger." [19]

Plan and Purpose of the Book

THIS BOOK, THEN, IS GROUNDED HISTORICALLY, PSYCHO-logically, theologically, and ecumenically in serious scholarship. But it is not a narrowly academic book in the conventional, least of all pejorative, sense. It is, rather, deliberately written to and for the laics of the Church without whom nothing will change.

For those who know a modicum of church history, it has always been this way — a powerful clergy descending into corruption until the much larger body of lay faithful in various ways rises up to push for change. The corrupt change, if they change at all, because holy men and women begin the work on their own and then seek like-minded co-operators, leading over time to a mass movement for change, sometimes even revolution-ary change. Such happened in the eleventh century with the Gregorian reforms; such happened in the sixteenth century with various European reformations and the Counter-Reformation at Trent; such happened again in the nineteenth century leading to dramatic changes at Vatican I. The Church is overdue for another period of major reform precisely if she is to survive and flourish anew in the twenty-first century. It is time for a dramatic series of structural changes. It is time for us to get to work. As the recent and controverted post-synodal exhortation puts it:

> Crises need to be faced together. This is hard, since persons sometimes withdraw in order to avoid saying what they feel; they retreat into a craven silence. At these times, it becomes all the more important to create opportunities for speaking heart to heart. (*Amoris Laetitia* no. 234)

If, speaking from our hearts, we boldly wish to advance lasting and significant change in the Church, it will be up to the laics to refuse

19 *Models of the Church* (Image Classics, 1991), 40.

any longer to be imprisoned by "craven silence" but instead to begin working toward the implementation of these changes, using the power of numbers, media persuasion, theological argumentation, and financial support (or its withholding) to force recalcitrant and in some cases wicked hierarchs to change.

Each chapter of this book presents necessary changes in ascending order of difficulty but *descending* order of importance. In other words, chapter two's proposed reforms will be both the easiest to implement and in many ways the most important, followed closely by chapter 3. I begin deliberately with the parish (ch. 2), and then proceed to the diocese (ch. 3) before looking at national or regional structures (ch. 4), and finally married clergy (ch. 5). I proceed in this fashion because I am convinced that the changes to parish governance would be the easiest and most straightforward to implement, meeting the least resistance and having the greatest interest. The parish is also, of course, the place where the vast majority of Catholics interact with the Church in an official and direct way; relatively few do so at the diocesan level, and fewer still at levels beyond that.

The changes proposed for the parish are mirrored in those proposed for the diocese. In a very real sense, if the changes of the first two chapters were implemented, the changes argued for in the remaining three chapters would be of relatively lesser importance and urgency. For the key structural units of the Church remain the parish and diocese, and if the modes of governance of both are reformed along the lines of what is suggested here, and if the Catholic imaginary (discussed in the first chapter) is reconceived to dethrone the near-idolatrous centralized papacy of the last two hundred years, then the Church will already by that point be on far more secure grounds.

There is an additional logic that undergirds the structure of this book and that may be conceived in terms of human costs. What is asked of people in the second chapter is only a little beyond what they already do in most places. What is asked in the third and fourth chapters would require considerably more work and, in the third chapter at least, a considerably larger number of people. And what is proposed in the fifth and final chapter is arguably the costliest change here proposed, which is why it is last, that is, of relatively lowest priority. It is also, as

I shall show, the change that will have serious implications for a large number of people not currently involved in the Church in this way, whose voices are often overlooked: those of women and children. The fifth chapter, then, proceeds with the most caution and takes pains to recognize that the change proposed here will involve very serious sacrifices that can often be difficult to make.

Each chapter will follow the same format: introduction; description of current practice and its problems; and then an elaboration of the changes, showing their justificatory roots in history and theology, ancient and modern. Let me note here that the very practical proposals put forth in each chapter are deliberately left loose, and for two reasons. First, I abhor micro-management. Consequently, having sketched out the broad changes that need to happen, and having given Catholics the background and reassurance to know that all the proposals here are *entirely orthodox* and have abundant theological and historical justification, I have opted not to go further and specify very particular practices or offer very finely grained details — e.g., how many members should be elected to a parish council, and how should they be elected. Those things can be worked out in particular contexts as people find what works best, within a broad framework, for their unique parish or diocese.

This takes me to my second reason for sketching out some possibilities but then backing off. I want to respect the status of the Latin Church as an autonomous sister church with more than enough adults to decide many of the broad details my proposals will require for their proper execution.[20] Following the principle of subsidiarity — too rarely and too little invoked in ecclesiology — those closest to the situation should figure out how to implement these proposals.

But before we can even think of those proposals and consider them in some detail, we need to spend some time thinking about how we have thought about and conceived the Church in the modern period, which I date from the reign of Pope Pius VII (1800–1823). In other words, perhaps the most important task at the start of our long journey of reform is a psychological and conceptual one. We

---

20 For more on this see the short but invaluable article by John Faris, "The Latin Church *Sui Iuris*," *The Jurist* 62 (2002): 280–93.

must honestly interrogate what I shall call the "Catholic imaginary," in which paternal projections and misplaced longings for authoritative father figures relieving us of our own responsibilities have come to do very real harm to Catholics and to the Church. Thus my first chapter, drawing on psychoanalytic thought, argues for reconceiving notions of spiritual paternity and obedience. Absent such a thoroughgoing re-examination — at once psychological and theological — of how we conceive of popes, bishops, and priests (that is, of all those Catholics usually call "father") parts of this book may prove somewhat difficult for some people to conceive of doing. That said, let me advise the reader that this is the most theoretically dense chapter. For those who want to get to the practical ideas first, and perhaps need less convincing psychologically as to the value of those practical changes, I suggest skipping straight to chapter 2.

Chapter 2 begins closest to home, at the parish level, arguing that the laics have a right and responsibility to play in governing their parish on equal terms as the clergy. The changes here would not be enormous nor necessarily immediate, but would be significant over the long-term. Parish councils will be required in all parishes with the laics having both voice and vote over finances, parish policies and procedures, and the appointment and removal of clergy. No longer will priests control parishes entirely on their own. What is proposed is not a "takeover" by the laics but a new model in which priest and people hold each other accountable. This model of the "one" and the "many" is deeply Trinitarian at heart, and is the only icon, the only image, the only model for ecclesial governance at all levels that makes theological sense.[21]

Chapters 3 and 4 argue for similar changes at the diocesan and national levels, and these would be major structural alterations to how the Latin Church is governed. At both levels, what would be created would be both full and standing synods so that the task of governing a diocese now involves the laics and clergy having both voice and vote in matters of policy (not doctrine) and election, including the election

---

21   For more in Trinitarian icons of the Church, see Radu Bordeianu's splendid book *Dumitru Staniloae: An Ecumenical Ecclesiology* (Bloomsbury, 2013).

of bishops. The national conferences of bishops, in turn, would be reconstituted so that, like one finds in some Eastern Churches today, these conferences would become real, full, and properly functioning synods, again having legislative and electoral powers. As I asked more than ten years ago now, if synods and synodal elections are permitted to Eastern Catholics, why are they denied to Latin Catholics?[22]

Chapter 5 is deliberately last because it is too often the idea that lazy and unimaginative people leap to *first* when contemplating Catholic reforms today. In this chapter I argue cautiously in favor of rethinking mandatory celibacy not just for priests but — going beyond what I have argued elsewhere[23] very recently — even for *bishops*. This chapter builds on another book of mine finished just this year on the question of married clergy, but here it goes beyond even that to raise the question of whether the Church needs to think about returning to the very early practice of a married episcopate. To do so will require rethinking the size of most Latin dioceses today. I shall propose that dioceses be much smaller and more numerous. Only in this way could they be administered on a human scale by a man having a human family. His human paternity will then come to undergird, and in some very real ways protect, his spiritual paternity, a concept that has too often been vacuous and unhelpfully abstract, allowing many bishops, as we have seen in Pennsylvania, California, New York, and elsewhere, callously to disregard the profound pain and deep damage done to sexually abused children.[24] The disappearance of the humanity of the victims in the eyes of bishops has been one of the most hideous of many egregious outbreaks in this crisis without end.

---

22 See my "Look to Tradition: The Case for Electing Bishops," *Commonweal*, March 19, 2007, https://www.commonwealmagazine.org/look-tradition.

23 See my *Married Catholic Priests*, in press with the University of Notre Dame Press.

24 Perhaps the most appalling example of this — it's a long and competitive list — comes in a recent NPR story about bishops in Los Angeles shunting predatory priests into immigrant communities because, they said, "'there is no need to take corrective action, because folks who were undocumented won't report.'" "Immigrant Communities Were the 'Geographic Solution' to Predatory Priests," November 8, 2018: https://www.npr.org/2018/11/08/665251345/immigrant-communities-were-the-geographic-solution-to-predator-priests.

CHAPTER 1

Toward a Future
without Illusions

Introduction

AS THIS BOOK WAS TAKING SHAPE, THE CONVICTION GREW
that this chapter needed to be first in order to address head-on some of
the challenges to understanding and accepting the changes proposed in
the rest of the book. In other words, the changes proposed here depart
to such a degree from how Catholics have conceived of the Church,
and their role in it, as to be something of an intellectual or cognitive
chasm over which it may be difficult to cross unaided. This chapter,
then, constitutes a kind of psychological "bridge" to those changes.

The Catholic Imaginary

CATHOLICS NEED TO UNDERTAKE A MAJOR RECONFIGURA-
tion of what I shall call the modern Catholic imaginary. That phrase
is borrowed and adapted from the eminent Catholic philosopher
Charles Taylor.[1] In his book, *Modern Social Imaginaries*, he argues
that a social imaginary is to be found in the ways people imagine their
social existence: how their lives fit with others, how they expect the
world normally to operate, and how certain notions and images are
often presupposed in the composition of social life. An imaginary is
not an explicit social theory, but a tool that rules in or out certain types

---

1 There is some argument to be made that Taylor is not the originator of the
concept. It goes back to the controversial French psychoanalyst Jacques Lacan, but
was picked up and developed by the Franco-Greek philosopher and psychoanalyst
Cornelius Castoriadis in his 1975 book *L'Institution imaginaire de la société*.

of permissible questions, conceptions, and ideas about our social existence. The idea of an "imaginary" centers on "the way ordinary people 'imagine' their social surroundings, and this is often not expressed in theoretical terms, but carried in images, stories, and legends."[2]

The Catholic tradition is replete with images, stories, and legends. Churches are full (or once were) of images of saints, angels, and Christ. Stories abound, not just formalized in Scripture, but also and especially in the lives of the saints, of sisters and priests, of popes and bishops, living and dead. And some of those stories seem to cross over into what some would consider legends — that is, stories whose details may be incredible and fanciful to some degree.

The Catholic imaginary — the ways in which Catholics have conceived of themselves and of the Church, and their relationship with the Church — has changed over the ages. Broadly speaking, I would argue that the imaginary was, for most of Catholic history, minimal and local. All the larger imaginaries in which Catholics conceive themselves — nation-state, ethnic group, and "religion" — are creations of modernity, largely in the aftermath of the French Revolution.

As the Church moves from its confines in Western Europe, especially in the so-called age of discovery in which the Church expands on the coattails of various imperial powers moving into what would become Canada, the United States, and Latin America, the Catholic imaginary slowly begins to expand to take on a more international color. As new churches are planted, especially in the so-called new world, the imaginary of Catholics becomes more universalist in nature; and if the Church is increasingly found universally throughout the world, then the conception of a universal shepherd begins slowly to embed itself within the Catholic imaginary.

By the turn of the nineteenth century, the bishop of Rome is becoming that "universal shepherd" not just in actual fact, but very much in the center of the Catholic imaginary, which becomes now heavily centered on the images, ideas, and personages of the popes, about whom many legends and stories grow. Indeed, we can posit a direct

---

2 Charles Taylor, *Modern Social Imaginaries* (Durham, NC: Duke University Press, 2004), 23.

co-relation if not causation: the less the bishop of Rome remains narrowly tied to particular territory in the central Italian peninsula (where he rules like other European monarchs) known as the Papal States, the more he becomes willing to see an expansion of his role to become universal teacher of the nations.[3]

Modern technology will come greatly to aid this expansive new role. The telegraph allows newspapers to transmit the same story around the world, and those papers to be quickly transported by the railroads to far-flung parts of the Church. Lithographs and oleographs allow for cheap mass printing of images of the pope, which can increasingly be found around the world in Catholic homes in the nineteenth century. And cheap mass printing becomes the tool popes use to propagate their increasingly endless torrent of writings. By the end of the nineteenth century, the popes — as John O'Malley has recently documented — come to write an ever-increasing number of documents on a vast array of topics. If we start with Pope Pius VII (r. 1800–1823) we find that he published only one encyclical; Pius IX (1846–1878) published thirty-eight; and Leo XIII (1878–1903) seventy-five. Since then, popes published not just scores of encyclicals but all manner of documents — exhortations, homilies, letters, apostolic constitutions, speeches, and others — at ever-increasing length ranging over an exhausting array of topics. Pope Pius XII (r. 1939–1958) and John Paul II (r. 1978–2005) were especially loquacious.

These documents give the popes a prominence at the heart of the Catholic imaginary they never had during the first 1800 years of the Church. They become domineering father-figures both in the Catholic imaginary and in actual practice in the life of the Church. One of the many deleterious side-effects of this is the increasing infantilization of Catholics the world over, who find themselves impotent and unwilling to act without papal sanction and incentive in matters both small and large — as we saw with the American bishops in November 2018. The pope has now become not just another bishop, not even a "universal"

---

3 This is a thesis given ample documentation in histories of the papacy in the nineteenth century, especially those of John Pollard, Eamon Duffy, Owen Chadwick, and John O'Malley, all of them cited later in this book.

pastor and teacher, but the father of fathers who dominates each and every Catholic, watching over them and telling them what to do and think on an ever-increasing array of subjects.

No modern thinker has been more valuable in diagnosing the unhealthy fixation on papal father-figures than Sigmund Freud. I am aware that the Freudian tradition of analysis has fallen greatly from favor across the Western world, which is why it is precisely now that it can be re-appropriated since it has nothing to gain but still much to teach.[4] I am aware, too, that too many Christians have made fools of themselves by dismissing Freud without reading him. But, as I have shown elsewhere, such defensiveness and dismissiveness on the part of Christians cannot be justified.[5]

In learning from Freud and the tradition after him—especially in the British independent or middle school (Fairbairn, Winnicott, Guntrip, Coltart, and others)—as I have for more than a quarter-century now, I simply follow the method pioneered by the Church Fathers: "despoiling the Egyptians" (cf. Exodus 3:22).[6] We take and use what is good in Freud—and a thousand others, from Aristotle and Plato to Nietzsche and Marx—and leave behind what is not. That is the same method and rationale that leads me to argue, as I did above, for learning from Anglicans and other non-Catholics. It is profoundly *uncatholic,* a sign of a mean and ungenerous little mind, to refuse to learn or to accept certain ideas merely because of sniffy anxieties about their provenance.

---

4 In this I follow closely Adam Phillips: "This is certainly a good time for psycho-analysis: because it is so widely discredited, because there is no prestige, or glamour, or money in it, only those who are really interested will go into it. And now that Freud's words are so casually dismissed, a better, more eloquent case needs to be made for the value of his writing" ("After Strachey," *London Review of Books* 29 no. 19 [4 October 2007]: 36).

5 See my "We Have Nothing to Fear from Freud" in *Catholic Herald,* November 17, 2017: http://www.catholicherald.co.uk/issues/november-17th-2017/weve-nothing-to-fear-from-freud/. And see my "Orthodoxy and Freud: Is a Dialogue Possible?" *Orthodoxy in Dialogue,* November 21, 2017: https://orthodoxyindialogue.com/2017/11/21/ortho-doxy-and-freud-is-a-conversation-possible-by-a-a-j-deville/. A longer, fuller treatment is in the works in a book I am working on, tentatively titled "Theology after Freud."

6 An excellent overview of this method is found in Augustine Casiday's *Remember the Days of Old: Orthodox Thinking on the Patristic Heritage* (St. Vladimir's Seminary Press, 2014).

The Catholic is unafraid of learning from so-called pagans, atheists, and others, for he knows that the Spirit can plant seeds in ground that is sometimes more fertile than that found within the Church — something akin to what Justin Martyr and other Fathers called *logos spermatikos.*

In this way, Freud and psychoanalytic methods more generally are not just useful to Catholics but share the same goals for the liberation of the human person from neurotic illusion and idolatry. As William Wahl has written, "not only can we affirm that psychoanalysis and religion 'desire the same things,' we can also see that the psychoanalytic contribution to the aims of religion is substantial."[7] My use of psychoanalytic thought in this book is precisely because I see it as *helping* the Church by questioning the "often excessive or facile obedience" expected by and in the Church.[8]

At its best, psychoanalysis offers us an unflinching look at the two problems at the heart of the current crisis in the Catholic Church: sex and power, and the often-resultant idols we make of both, and the pathologies caused by unhealthful attachment to and exploitation of both.[9] Learning to think differently about both for the good of the Church will require — and be aided in part by — the "necessary destructions of psychoanalysis," as Christopher Bollas has phrased it.[10]

Many of us have been bred to avoid talking about both sex and power in something called "polite company." Such discussions — I have been told — are "crass" or "crude" or "vulgar." Such avoidance and such notions of politeness are just masks the bourgeoisie wear to hide their discomfort. Those masks have now been ripped off the face of the Church, and *we must thank God for that.* We must face these issues squarely, unflinchingly, and for as long as it takes so that we can ensure that they are not exploited and abused in the future on the same scale as the present. That is the very goal and hope of this book.

---

7 "Pathologies of Desire and Duty: Freud, Ricoeur, and Castoriadis on Transforming Religious Culture," *Journal of Religion and Health* 47 (2008): 399.

8 Ibid.

9 Adam Phillips addresses the connections between sex, belief, and idolatry in his essay "Psychoanalysis and Idolatry" in *On Kissing, Tickling, and Being Bored: Psychoanalytic Essays on the Unexamined Life* (Harvard University Press, 1993), 109–21.

10 Christopher Bollas, *The Mystery of Things* (Routledge, 1999), 27.

The Temptation and Problem of Catholic Idolatry

FREUD IS AT HIS BEST AND MOST USEFUL WHEN HE LOOKS at the human practice of creating idols and totems onto whom we project all sorts of longings and desires, good and bad, and in whom we purport to find "saviors" of various sorts before whose assumed messianic powers we often secretly like to prostrate ourselves because of unacknowledged and sometimes frankly masochistic desires (which sadistic and predatory priests, bishops, and cardinals are only too keen to take advantage of). Freud saw with greater insight than just about anybody of the last century the destructive power of idolatry and sexual abuse.

The term idolatry is one that Freud, as a lapsed but nonetheless deeply learned (if not religiously conflicted[11]) Jew, knew to be the worst sin that could be imagined by the people of Israel. As Adam Phillips has bluntly put it, Freud was a "man whose project was the destruction of idolatry."[12] For our part, Catholic Christians have made the mistake of assuming that we are free from such temptations, which must belong to the past and to some primitive peoples like those of Israel and its surrounding tribes. The universal Catechism shatters such illusions on our part:

> Idolatry not only refers to false pagan worship. *It remains a constant temptation to faith.* Idolatry consists in divinizing what is not God. Man commits idolatry whenever he honors and reveres a creature in place of God, whether this be gods or demons (for example, satanism), power, pleasure, race, ancestors, the state, money, etc.... Idolatry rejects the unique Lordship of God; it is therefore incompatible with communion with God. (no. 2113)

This view on the pervasiveness of idolatry is also echoed in *Lumen Fidei*:

---

11 See Ana-Maria Rizzuto, *Why Did Freud Reject God?* (Yale University Press, 1998) for a careful treatment of this question. She is an Argentinian-American Catholic and practicing psychoanalyst and psychiatrist.

12 Adam Phillips, *On Kissing*, 113.

The opposite of faith is shown to be idolatry. While Moses is speaking to God on Sinai, the people cannot bear the mystery of God's hiddenness, they cannot endure the time of waiting to see his face. Faith by its very nature demands renouncing the immediate possession which sight would appear to offer; it is an invitation to turn to the source of the light, while respecting the mystery of a countenance which will unveil itself personally in its own good time. Martin Buber once cited a definition of idolatry proposed by the rabbi of Kock: idolatry is "when a face addresses a face which is not a face." In place of faith in God, it seems better to worship an idol, into whose face we can look directly and whose origin we know. . . . Idols exist, we begin to see, as a pretext for setting ourselves at the centre of reality. (no. 13)

Idolatry "remains a constant temptation to faith" and a "pretext for setting ourselves at the centre of reality." I would say that the temptation to idolatry is far more insidious than Catholics realize, and that too often, within the structures of the Church, what we have set at the center of reality is the pope and bishops, not Jesus Christ (even as we claim they are His "vicars"). Thus idolatry is not extraneous to the Church at all, and Catholics are by no means immune to it. In fact, let it be said that idolatry has been *increasing* in the modern world and Church alike, and that the supposed "secularization" we keep hearing about is nothing other than a cover for covert idolatry.[13] This is perhaps most clearly illustrated in considering another passage from the catechism — from the Council of Trent this time:

Bishops and priests being, as they are, God's interpreters and ambassadors, empowered in His name to teach mankind the divine law and the rules of conduct, and holding, as they do, His place on earth, it is evident that no nobler function than

13 As Benjamin Fong says in his new book, *Death and Mastery: Psychoanalytic Drive Theory and the Subject of Late Capitalism* (Columbia University Press, 2018), "there is perhaps no more confused assertion, for a critical theorist, than that capitalist society is becoming increasingly 'secular'" (page 81).

theirs can be imagined. Justly, therefore, are they called not
only Angels, *but even gods*, because of the fact that they exercise in our midst the power and prerogatives of the immortal
God.[14] (my emphasis)

If this is encouraging Catholics to think of bishops and priests as
"even gods," then it is quite literally idolatry. Trent may be thought by
most Catholics (if they know of it at all) to be long gone; but, once
again, a crucial insight from Freud comes back to haunt us: forgotten ≠ gone. This idolatrous elevation of clergy lives on in the Church's
unconscious memory, and the proof of this, as Freud showed in his
1914 essay "Remembering, Repeating, and Working Through," comes
via our actions, repetitive actions, which reveal in part the contents of
otherwise inaccessible memories that have not been worked through.
The actions of Catholics for centuries now have been to treat popes,
bishops, and priests as quasi-idols at minimum.

I am not much bothered by Trent's outrageous claim precisely
because it is so brazen and blatant. Far more worrying are the forms
of idolatry that are not so brazen and explicit and therefore much
more dangerously powerful. The chief example here is that of the
papacy in the aftermath of the First Vatican Council, whose legacy,
as Congar said, "occasioned a cult of the pope and exaltation of
papal prerogatives."[15]

The papal cult has functioned in a semi-idolatrous fashion for
more than a century now. This is not a terribly new or original insight.
Freud and more recent Christian commentators indebted to him[16]
have been stressing the necessity of recognizing idolatry in the lives
of "religious" people for nearly a century. As Paul Ricoeur put it more
than forty years ago:

14 Part II, "The Sacrament of Holy Orders: the Dignity of this Sacrament." Cited
in the on-line translation found here: http://www.saintsbooks.net/books/The%20
Roman%20Catechism.pdf.

15 Yves Congar, *I Believe in the Holy Spirit* (New York: Crossroad, 1997), 161.

16 See MacIntyre's *Ethics in the Conflicts of Modernity: An Essay on Desire, Practical
Reasoning, and Narrative* (Cambridge University Press, 2016), esp. pp. 35–37. See also
his 1958 book *The Unconscious: A Conceptual Analysis* (rep. 1994 by Routledge), where
he speaks of "Freud's essential and unassailable greatness" (p. 46).

> There is a danger that believers may sidestep his radical ques-
> tioning of religion under the pretext that Freud is merely
> expressing the unbelief of scientism and his own agnosti-
> cism; but there is also the danger that unbelievers may con-
> fuse psychoanalysis with this unbelief and agnosticism. My
> working hypothesis . . . is that psychoanalysis is necessarily
> iconoclastic . . . and that this "destruction" of religion can be
> the counterpart of a faith *purified of all idolatry.*[17]

The purification of idolatry that must happen first and foremost in
the Catholic imaginary today is that centered around the figure of the
father—the holy father in Rome, the "most reverend father" in the
person of the bishop, and the father-pastor of the local parish. These
images and idols are not only psychologically destructive and theologically perverse: they have also played a direct and large role in the
ongoing sex abuse crisis. Before we get to that, let us examine the history
of how these images and idols entered the modern Catholic imaginary.

Current Problematic Practices and Concepts

THE CURRENT ENTIRELY CENTRALIZED CONCEPTION OF
papal and episcopal authority and control in the Church is not only
scarcely a century old (and thus hardly "traditional") but it lacks theological justification. It was, in large measure, the product of emergency
measures in a time of crisis—the aftermath of the French and other
European revolutions of 1789–1848.[18] That time has long since passed,
and the revolutionary threats have also disappeared, but the structures of
extreme papal centralization developed in their wake have not changed.
As so often happens throughout church history, events lead to solutions
that work in particular contexts, but those solutions often do not change
when the context and issues do, leading to a sclerotic structure in the
church that has outlived its usefulness. This is the law of unintended

---

17 *Freud and Philosophy: An Essay on Interpretation,* trans. P. Savage (Yale University Press, 1977), 230; my emphasis.

18 For more on this see Owen Chadwick's *The Popes and European Revolution*
(Oxford University Press, 1981).

consequences at work; and in papal, and, more generally, ecclesial history, we see this law doing damage numerous times before the Church finally makes long overdue adjustments. Sometimes the inherently conservative nature of institutions in general, and the Catholic Church in particular, is profoundly unhelpful and self-destructive. Too often ecclesial structures need to be nimble where they are heavy-laden.[19]

Now is the time for throwing off the heavy and cumbersome structures of the past which have aided and abetted the current crisis — and will prolong it if they are not changed. Pius VII seized power in his own revolutionary ways to get rid of the French episcopate appointed at Napoleon's behest and to name an entirely new bench of bishops — something no pope had ever done. In some ways, the unintended consequences of this are with us still, even though the precipitating threat died with Napoleon in 1821.

Nearly fifty years later, Rome had not forgotten the trauma, and so instituted at Vatican I a relatively conservative definition of primacy and infallibility that immediately gave way to a maximalist application. Vatican I, long recognized by all serious commentators as being restrained and rather conservative in its texts, spawned the bloated eminence of the modern papacy. Indeed, the legacy of Vatican I lingers in the Catholic imaginary, playing on certain unconscious assumptions (never articulated, let alone theologically justified, for they could not be) that the decrees of Vatican I somehow give the pope license to appoint bishops (and do many other unprecedented and unjustified things like dismantle the Latin liturgy[20]) without any kind of widespread consultation and accountability before, during, or after. If, *de jure*, Vatican I

19 That said, as I have demonstrated elsewhere, the Catholic Church since the early 1980s has proven itself more agile than many realize in being able, often relatively quickly, to devise new structures — ordinariates, prelatures, and the like — to respond to new situations. For details and discussion, see my "The Principles of Accommodation and Forgetting in the Twenty-First Century," in John Chryssavgis, ed., *Primacy in the Church: The Office of Primate and the Authority of Councils,* 2 vols. (Crestwood, NY: St. Vladimir's Seminary Press, 2016), II: 473–92.

20 I have long accepted the Ratzinger thesis that a pope dismantling the Latin liturgy and replacing it with a concoction devised by a dodgy commission (details of which are given in Louis Bouyer's memoirs) was not only an unprecedented papal power grab and so wrong in itself, but that its effects were and are deeply destructive of the Western Church's life.

is very limited and conservative in nature, *de facto* its reception into and influence upon the mind of the Church has been anything but. A minimalist decree has been given a maximalist interpretation and application — as Jean-Marie Roger Tillard rightly argued many years ago.[21] Certain images and ideas of papal power have been allowed to grow up after the council in justification of extreme innovations that popes would never have imagined. The canons of Vatican I held the tide against the worst of ultramontane floods; but those dams have long since been breached quite willingly by many prelates in the Church after the council to make an ostentatious display of sycophantic support of the supposedly beleaguered papal "prisoner of the Vatican."

And that is the problem with the First Vatican Council — which also, admittedly, afflicts many other councils before and since: the letter of its decrees ultimately matters far less than the narrative, canons, and practices constructed afterwards that make up much of the Catholic imaginary of post-conciliar years. That imaginary continues a subterranean existence just below the surface where it can wreak maximum havoc, suppressing all minimalist interpretations of Vatican I and making the maximalist ideas the only conscious "available-believables" in the Catholic imaginary.[22]

We are, it is devoutly to be hoped, now approaching the dissolution of this Catholic imaginary; for we now have overwhelming and incontrovertible evidence that the father-figures of clergy, including the pope, care very little for the welfare — physical, sexual, and above all

---

21 See his "The Jurisdiction of the Bishop of Rome," *Theological Studies* 40 (1979): 3–22; and, more generally, *Church of Churches: An Ecclesiology of Communion* (Michael Glazier, 1980).

22 Though I have here focused really only on the last two centuries, a significant argument could be made, drawing on Susan Wessel's superlative study *Leo the Great and the Spiritual Rebuilding of a Universal Rome* (Brill, 2008), that attempts at creating an imaginary around the papacy go all the way back to Pope Leo I who, presiding over the collapse of the Roman Empire in the West, begins (as his name-sake successor Leo XIII would do at the end of the nineteenth century) to conceive of the papacy in new ways, having now "spiritual" and "apostolic" authority to replace the authority he lost when the capital was moved in 330 to Constantinople and still more when the Western Empire fell apart. More recent studies, e.g., by George Demacopolous, also shed light on this phenomenon: see his *The Invention of Peter: Apostolic Discourse and Papal Authority in Late Antiquity* (University of Pennsylvania Press, 2016).

spiritual — of the children of the Church. They are, in fact, anti-fathers. If fathers are supposed to give, guide, and protect life, too many of the father-figures of the Church, above all bishops, have covered up the destruction of innocent life, or themselves violated innocent lives of children, seminarians, and others. The willingness to trust these father-figures with the welfare of children has now been revealed as an horrific mistake, destroying thousands of lives and permanently damaging many more. Now that the cover-up of clerical abuse has been revealed, it is clear that no clerics within the Catholic Church should ever again be put on pedestals and allowed to penetrate the unconscious Catholic mind (to say nothing, alas, of the rest of the body), as "fathers."

If the sex abuse crisis has done nothing else, it has torn the mask off these clerics to reveal them to be nothing more or other than human beings, although in some cases exceptionally depraved ones whose capacity for evil has been aided and abetted precisely by their "sovereignty" and lack of accountability to others. If this crisis is to be overcome by the Church, then we must continue to fully demythologize the clerical order. Let no cleric — especially if he be pope — ever again be idealized or, worse, idolized. Let us ever be on our guard to stamp out "papolatry" whenever it breaks out, honestly admitting that it is not just a crude slogan of Protestant polemics, but really does exist in the Catholic imaginary — and, I submit, on a far more widespread scale than most would admit.[23]

The modern (that is from 1800 onward) Catholic imaginary has been developed very largely by popes aware of the political precariousness of their position in revolutionary Europe (not just after 1789 in France, but after 1848 in much of the rest of Europe) and very much in need of psychological and financial support[24] from Catholics around the world, especially from the developing and increasingly rich and powerful New

---

23 How else to explain, e.g., the fact that Pope John Paul II's funeral was one of the largest such gatherings in history? How does one understand the millions who turn out for such events as World Youth Day? Nothing — *nothing* — gained there is unavailable at home: sacraments, catechesis, fellowship can all be had at home. The only purpose in going is, as all those who have gone tell me, "to see the pope" — not Jesus but the pope.

24 See John Pollard's fascinating and indispensable book *Money and the Rise of the Modern Papacy: Financing the Vatican, 1850–1950* (Cambridge University Press, 2008).

World. As Eamon Duffy[25] and others have demonstrated, and as John O'Malley's new book[26] confirms in detail, popes from Pius VI onward were very adept at building up contacts with Catholics on a seemingly personal level; and all his successors increasingly exploited this via every new technology that came along. The First Vatican Council both grew out of but then greatly aided this process immeasurably, leading O'Malley to conclude that its chief result is "a strikingly new prominence in Catholic consciousness for the ordinary believer." Such believers were led by the hierarchs to think that "personal devotion to the pope became a new Catholic virtue."[27]

Every pope since then has exploited this pseudo-virtue, having more and more tools at his disposal with which to do so. If nineteenth-century popes were confined to the printing press, telegraph, and railway, soon their twentieth-century successors were given the radio, the telephone, and then the television; and their successors now have websites, Youtube channels, Twitter, Facebook, and other social media. This mass media, when married to mass transport — especially the advent of the car and then the airplane — has allowed popes to start traveling beyond Rome to insert themselves more deeply into the imaginations of Catholics worldwide, which they have done to extensive and alarming degrees. Pius XII, while still cardinal secretary of state, was the first to begin international travels, but it was Paul VI (1963–1978) who began the deplorable habit of jetting around the world to be parachuted into various places to massive adoring crowds, usually at enormous expense to local churches that could ill afford it. (Often the local churches were saddled with the costs — security, food, accommodations, transportation — for papal trips, and often these ran into the millions of dollars, inflicting debt on poorer countries requiring decades to repay.[28])

---

25 *Saints and Sinners: A History of the Popes,* 4th ed. (Yale University Press, 2015).

26 *Vatican I: The Council and the Making of the Ultramontane Church* (Harvard University Press, 2018).

27 Ibid., 240.

28 To give just one recent example, the Irish press are reporting that Pope Francis's 36-hour jaunt to Ireland in August 2018 cost almost a million Euros *per hour*: thirty-two million Euros, to be precise, twenty million of which will come from local parishes and dioceses in Ireland, which is to say the Irish people: https://www.irishcentral.com/news/pope-francis-ireland-cost.

All these papal machinations and forms of self-promotion would not have gotten very far were it not for the perversely willing behavior of too many bishops around the world, including especially those from the Americas. This behavior has only been picked up, amplified, and mindlessly copied by bishops the world over since the end of the nineteenth century, thereby proving the French Catholic theorist René Girard's famous idea of mimetic desire to be correct: I learn to desire in part by observing what others desire and imitating that and them.[29] Once bishops in America in the late-nineteenth century began flogging their desire to be ruled by Rome, others followed suit.

It was not always that way, whether in America or for many more centuries before that in other parts of the world. As one current American bishop has documented, his predecessors in the American episcopate had, from the founding of the first dioceses in this country, a regular habit of meeting in council to decide their own affairs with scant contact with, let alone direct input from, the pope.[30] It was only in conjunction with the loss of the Papal States and the rise of the self-pitying campaign of Pius IX as "prisoner of the Vatican"[31] that bishops in the Americas and elsewhere started ostentatiously showing their support for the pope by conveniently letting him do their jobs for them.[32] Only in this period do we start to see the popes

29 See especially book III, chapter 1, of Girard's *Things Hidden Since the Foundation of the World*, trans. Stephen Bann and Michael Metteer (Stanford University Press, 1987). For a more direct application to theology, see part I, chapter 3, of Girard's *The One by Whom Scandal Comes*, trans. Malcolm B. DeBevoise (Michigan State University Press, 2014).

30 Timothy Dolan, "The Bishops in Council," *First Things* (April 2005): https://www.firstthings.com/article/2005/04/the-bishops-in-council.

31 The phrase has long been a staple of the literature of the nineteenth-century papacy. It is used more recently in David Kertzer's two insightful books: *Prisoner of the Vatican* (Houghton Mifflin Harcourt, 2004); and *The Pope Who Would Be King: The Exile of Pius IX and the Emergence of Modern Europe* (Random House, 2018).

32 Most curiously in the same timeframe, but in the Anglican world, there were "colonial" bishops in North America and elsewhere in the British Empire who, like their Roman brethren, wanted voluntarily to surrender their nascent powers and instead be ruled by the "head office." These bishops wanted England and its Parliament to pass legislation restricting the electoral and legislative powers of newly emergent synods in the colonies, subjecting them to centralized control from London. On this see Harry Huskins, "A Very Different Communion: Failed Attempts in the 1850s to

muscling in on the appointment of local bishops rather than their being locally elected, *and bishops allowing—nay, encouraging—that to happen.* Why is that?

One of the recurring themes in Freud's work from his penultimate period (1919 to 1927) is the complicated relationship human beings have to authority, especially authority that either is divine, or makes claims to know and teach about the divine. In his 1919 essay "A Child is Being Beaten," 1924's "The Economic Problem of Masochism," and above all his 1927 book *The Future of an Illusion,* Freud saw again and again in his patients, and in cultures at large, the secret craving some people have for omnipotent paternal authority figures to both dominate them and to rescue them.[33] This need not rise to the level of an explicit "perversion" (to use Freud's word) or sexual fantasy: "doubt remains . . . whether the phantasy ought to be described as purely 'sexual,' nor can one venture to call it 'sadistic.'"[34] But no doubt remained for Freud based on his clinical examples that this craving finds its "origin in an . . . attachment to the father."[35]

That attachment, though it may superficially appear to be, in the case of men, self-emasculating, actually can hide a form of what Freud called "moral masochism." Moral masochism typically involves the placing of the self at the disposal of "impersonal powers"[36] (the papacy of the nineteenth century being an extremely clear example of such). In other words, there is some kind of psychological need that is felt and met by surrendering one's own responsibilities and powers to another,

Regulate the Colonial Church by Imperial Statute," *Journal of the Canadian Church Historical Society* 52 (2014): 51–82.

33 Those who are inclined to dismiss all this as outdated nonsense from a long-dead man of dubious ideas would do well to recall that in 2015 the sadomasochistic novel *Fifty Shades of Grey* burst onto the scene as the "fastest selling adult novel of all time," selling more than 125 *million copies* and being translated into more than fifty languages before being turned into a movie that made more than half a *billion* dollars at the box-office. See Zoe Williams, "Why Women Love 50 Shades of Grey," *The Guardian,* July 6, 2012.

34 Ethel Spector Person, ed., *On Freud's 'A Child is Being Beaten'* (Routledge, 2013), 187.

35 Ibid., 198.

36 "The Economic Problem of Masochism," reprinted in *Essential Papers on Masochism,* ed. M. A. F. Hanly (New York University Press, 1995), 279.

especially if that other happens to be a domineering paternal figure as, by all accounts, Pius IX was.[37] Among his other charming virtues, he ridiculed mercilessly his "enemies," that is, other bishops, during Vatican I for not voting the way he wanted, and openly threatened[38] to send them all home and define papal infallibility and universal jurisdiction by himself, without conciliar mandate, as he had arrogantly decided to do sixteen years earlier in defining the Immaculate Conception. Many bishops were so distraught by the abuse that they quietly left Rome before the end of the council in July; nearly a quarter were gone before the final vote that month.

The search and longing for father-figures is the central psychological desire exploited by the modern papacy and aided by the modern episcopate, leading to the modern Catholic imaginary in which the pope is omnipotent, omniscient, and omnipresent. While one could cite mid-century[39] practices — e.g., the fawning language of *L'Osservatore Romano* when it conveyed every papal statement as though from an oracle on high, or carting the pope about on a *sedia gestatoria* like some ancient emperor or medieval potentate, an image rendered all the more acute (and theologically offensive) by his wearing a tiara whose imposition at his coronation was accompanied by proclaiming him the "father of princes and kings and rulers of the world"[40] — there are perhaps even more disturbing, and certainly more numerous, examples the closer we get to our own day.

37 See not just John O'Malley's book directly, but the sources it cites for Pius's biography. But especially see T. A. Howard, *The Pope and the Professor: Pius IX, Ignaz von Dollinger, and the Quandary of the Modern Age* (Oxford University Press, 2017). For a superlative study of the larger context, with chapters on Pius IX, see Owen Chadwick's *A History of the Popes 1830–1914* (Oxford University Press, 1998).

38 See John O'Malley, *Vatican I*, 186.

39 Or earlier: the wonderfully acerbic English priest and scholar Adrian Fortescue, in a letter — note well — written in 1910 denounced the fact that "Centralisation grows and goes madder every century. Even at Trent they hardly foresaw this kind of thing. Does it really mean that one cannot be a member of the Church of Christ without being, as we are, absolutely at the mercy of an Italian lunatic?" A decade later, under a different but even more busybody pope, Benedict XV, Fortescue, again in a letter to a friend then visiting Rome, asked, "By the way, will you give a message from me to the Roman Ordinary? Tell him to look after his own diocese and not to write any more Encyclicals."

40 For evidence see this video clip of the coronation of Pope Pius XII in 1939: https://www.youtube.com/watch?v=QbY-yg729MQ.

To be sure, one could argue, with some justice, that Pope Paul VI eliminated a lot of these medieval court trappings — though he was crowned and carted about on that neo-imperial throne above the heads of the masses — and that his successor, Pope John Paul I, in his thirty-three days as bishop of Rome, seems finally — and thankfully — to have killed off the whole notion of a coronation and all its appurtenances. Those are helpful though limited blows against the idolatry of the papacy in the Catholic imaginary.

But at the same time, the papacy was inserting itself ever more insidiously into the life of Catholics the world over. The same pope, Paul VI, who tried to rein in some appearances of a medieval court, is the one who began the deplorable and entirely unnecessary habit of jetting off around the world to be fawned over by politicians at the United Nations in New York and by Catholics in far-flung parts of the globe. Have these Catholics no local successors to the apostles to preach to them? What is the purpose of the pope coming if not to further cement his place in the Catholic imaginary? There is nothing he does on these visits — give speeches, celebrate Mass, draw attention to issues of peace and reconciliation — that cannot be done at far less cost by local church leaders.

Far, far worse than his propensity for treating the entire world as his diocese was his massive hijacking of the Latin liturgy after the council and his inflicting enormously damaging (Ratzinger's words) liturgical reforms on the entire Western Church. That one action constitutes such a massive papal power-grab as had never been seen in 2000 years.[41] Paul also continued to take unto himself the apparent right to write letters to the entire world on a variety of topics.

All this, and more, would continue under his successors, leading me by October of 2013 to write an article almost begging people to tune him out.[42] My appeal, of course, accomplished nothing, as everybody continued to hang on his every word.

---

41 Louis Bouyer's memoirs give the goods away on this catastrophe and its aetiology: *The Memoirs of Louis Bouyer: From Youth and Conversion to Vatican II, the Liturgical Reform, and After*, trans. John Pepino (Angelico Press, 2015).

42 https://www.realclearreligion.org/articles/2013/10/16/who_cares_what_the_pope_says.html.

Even in the dark and dolorous days of 2018, as the sex abuse crisis continued relentlessly to unfold, clearly implicating the pope, many continued mindlessly to defend him in sycophantic ways. Consider, briefly, three examples — the first from some laics, the second from a well-known and influential priest, and the third from two entire groups of bishops.

This first example is without doubt the clearest manifestation I have seen of cringe-worthy and nauseatingly infantilizing language with clear masochistic undertones. In this petition to the pope,[43] we read the following (with my emphasis):

> *Holy Father*, we want to affirm the love we have for you as the Successor of St. Peter, for Catholics in every time and place possess a unique *filial* love and *reverence towards the person of the Holy Father*. With all our hearts we desire that he who fills the Petrine Office be defended from anything that would harm his person or the effectiveness of his ministry.
>
> *   *   *
>
> Therefore, as the *sheep* entrusted to your care by the Good Shepherd, conscious of our authority as *children* of God the Father who have been purchased by the Blood of His beloved Son, we ask for an immediate, full and exhaustive investigation be made into these allegations so that the moral witness of your person, and that of the senior hierarchy of the Church, may be exonerated of all suspicion of incompetence, neglect, and evildoing.
>
> We ask that this investigation be conducted by persons whose authority, neutrality, and moral witness, be universally self-evident, so that its exoneration of you, Holy Father, will be effective in restoring your person and the *sacred Office* you hold to the Church and to the world.
>
> With profound *filial* love,
> Your *Children* in Christ

43 https://www.popefrancispetition.com.

This revolting letter, in its imagery, tone, and content perfectly captures the Catholic imaginary as it surrounds the pope. One could, being charitable, perhaps write all this off as an excessive deference on the part of theologically unsophisticated and developmentally arrested people. But how then to explain similar, if slightly more restrained, claims and language from priests and bishops? The priest in question is Thomas Rosica, one of the official media spokesmen for the Vatican. On the Latin calendar's feast of St. Ignatius of Loyola, he published "The Ignatian Qualities of the Petrine Ministry of Pope Francis" in which he claimed that

> Pope Francis breaks Catholic traditions whenever he wants because he is "free from disordered attachments." Our Church has indeed entered a new phase: with the advent of this first Jesuit pope, it is openly ruled by an individual rather than by the authority of Scripture alone or even its own dictates of tradition plus Scripture.[44]

Nowhere in Vatican I or any other authoritative source has the Church *ever* so much as *hinted* that it is ruled by an "individual rather than by the authority of Scripture alone."

Not to be outdone, the entire episcopal conference of England and Wales recently returned from its regular (*ad limina*) visit to Rome, after which it issued this statement, which revealingly begins with a little self-emasculation and cringing before the papal throne: "We asked the Holy Father for a message which we could bring back to our dioceses, to our priests and people." (Is the message of Jesus Christ in the gospels insufficient?) The statement continues:

> As we spoke with Pope Francis we realised, more and more, that he . . . is indeed gifted with a unique grace of the Holy Spirit of God. Even in this time of turmoil, the Holy Father is so clearly rooted in God and blessed by God. His peace is

---

44 http://saltandlighttv.org/blogfeed/getpost.php?id=72516

secure. His life is serene. We know, because he showed us his
heart. It is the heart of a loving father.[45]

All these are not just bad theology, but bad (paternalistic, passive)
psychology as well. Nevertheless, they are clear and consistent examples of the role of the papacy in the Catholic imaginary today. On
a reduced scale, this imaginary conceives the relationship between
bishops and priests in very similar terms. All three are fathers. If the
pope is sometimes addressed as "Most Holy Father," bishops are "Most
Reverend Father" and priests "Reverend Father."

Such language has had the effect of paralyzing people, making
them passive and undermining any thoughts of action through guilt
born of neurotic ideas of patricidal disloyalty. How else to explain
the unwillingness of—to cite the most egregious example nearest
to hand—the American bishops in November 2018 to take even the
pathetically inadequate actions they had proposed when a bizarre
late-night phone call from Rome bid them to stand down and take
no action at all? The effect of this was to reduce bishops once more
to the role of the pope's postmen (in Bismarck's apt phrase) waiting
on him to send them more letters telling them what to do, a pathetic
and degrading spectacle that invites recollection of Sergius Bulgakov's
claim about bishops at Vatican I indulging in "collective suicide."[46]

All this language, these notions, these concepts, must be re-thought as
part of analyzing and then draining the papal-centric Catholic imaginary.
Just as one recognizes that mere paternity is insufficient to make one into
a real father so, too, must it be noted that neither does mere ordination
confer paternal authority. It is possible to earn it, and thus for people
to come to recognize and even freely and legitimately to call certain
men their "spiritual father" after years of close, careful, constructive
relationship of being built up and not destroyed. But the conferral of all
such titles (including "holy father") should by no means be automatic.

---

45 Ad Limina Final Statement of October 1, 2018: http://www.catholicnews.org.
uk/Home/News/2018/Ad-Limina-Final-Statement
46 Sergius Bulgakov, "Le dogme du Vatican," *Le messager orthodoxe* 6 (1959): 25.
Bulgakov is widely thought to have been the most important and influential Russian
Orthodox theologian of the last century.

When Christ says "call no man father," for we have but one father and he is in heaven dwelling invisibly, I would argue that Christ (long before Freud) was aware of the dangers of human psychology. Those dangers are such that we need to be extremely careful about projecting on to God the Father images and expectations from our early experience of "fathers," whether biological or ecclesial. It is too easy for the mind, often in unconscious ways we rarely come to perceive (except, as Freud would later suggest, largely through our repeated, and typically unhealthy, actions[47]), to subtly equate parts of our earthly paternal experiences with expectations of how our heavenly Father is and how He treats us.

What we need now more than ever is for the Church to be purified and purged of paternalistic titles, images, and practices; we need a campaign of welcome and necessary iconoclasm, dismantling false images and powerful pretentions of popes and other papas or fathers in the Catholic imaginary, but also directly in the governance of the Church. Here, to be sure, I am *not* talking about their vital sacramental role—in, e.g., celebrating the Eucharist, or forgiving sins, or in ordinations—but rather the psychological role they play in the Catholic imaginary. Their sacramental role is integral to the Church's very nature and cannot be touched.

What Is to Be Done?

IN HIS EXTRAORDINARY NEW *TOUR DE FORCE* JUST PUB-lished last year, *Belief after Freud,* the Spanish Jesuit theologian and psychoanalyst Carlos Dominguez-Morano has argued that one of the key lessons of the earthly life of Jesus vis-à-vis his parents, especially revealed in the incident (Luke 2:41ff.) where they find him teaching in the temple at the age of twelve, is that He shows us how to overcome the problem of earthly fathers and their claims to power over us, which we then often internalize and project back onto other figures. This whole process is broken by Jesus, who shows us the importance of breaking it in our lives too: "Any type of paternal projection on

---

47 See his essay "Remembering, Repeating, and Working Through" in vol. 12 of the Strachey *Standard Edition* (1950): 145–57. The original was published in 1914.

other social figures must be overcome. Nobody on earth can claim paternal authority. Nobody can exert paternal power or protection functions in the Christian community."[48] The revelation of God in Christ shows us that the Father from whom Jesus proceeds, whom he manifests to the world, is a father who does not dominate his own son. Neither does the Father come to domineer as lord over us, but as friend who relates to and with us. For the Christian, then, the best way to conceive of how to relate to God, and to each other in the Church, is as friend-friend, not as father-son/father-daughter. For this is the very model that Christ gives when he says

> You are my friends if you do what I command you. No longer do I call you servants, for the servant does not know what his master is doing; but I have called you friends, for all that I have heard from my Father I have made known to you. (John 15:14–15)

Those who are called to be friends with God, as we all are, must learn to conceive him in those terms, moving past paternal projections and long-ings (often disguised and misdirected) and all the problems inherent in those. Thus Dominguez-Morano can say that "the Christian should not nostalgically search and long for the father. The father figure dwelling in the psyche of the person must be buried."[49] In doing so, we are following the model of Jesus, who, though calling Him Father, showed that He was free of any fear of, conflict with, or neurotic lingering resentment towards his Father. Jesus, having been free(d) of those issues, calls us to such freedom and autonomy as well. Once the paternal image and authority is buried, Dominguez-Morano counsels, it must not be res-urrected by us in the secret and perverse ways we so often do. To do so is to pervert the nature of the Church as a gathering of friends. In the

> Christian community, it has to be stated, in terms of clear psy-choanalytic reference, that *the place of the father should remain*

---

48 *Belief after Freud,* 162–63.
49 Ibid., 164.

empty. Father, teacher, or director are *not* Christian words insofar as they are used to describe a type of interpersonal relationship inside the community. *Only God can take that place.*[50]

For too long, the Catholic imaginary has claimed that God is in fact represented, or worse still embodied in the person of the "holy father, the pope of Rome" and in all others ordained to priestly rank who thereby gain the title "father." For a Christian to call any other Christian "father" is to destroy the relationship Christ embodied and came to show: "A relationship in which somebody would claim to be father or teacher to the believer would mean a relationship in which the *radical equality* we are called to would be under attack."[51]

And yet, alas, in the Church that equality has been under attack from the very beginning (cf. the dialogue between Jesus and the mother of the sons of Zebedee in Matt. 20:20–28). Too quickly the Church began setting up structures, and as Francis Dvornik and others famously showed, those structures were modeled on the authoritarian and hierarchical structures of the Roman army and empire.[52] Indeed, some of the language we take for granted today—diocese, province, metropolitan—is directly borrowed from the empire; other concepts, like that of holy "orders," mimic closely the sequential advancement of office holders in the Roman army.[53] This, as Dominguez-Morano rightly says, is very problematic because it means the Church has not merely become modeled after, but has herself become an "authoritarian system" in which "domination . . . fear, and feelings of guilt quite alien to Jesus of Nazareth's message and to what his message should inspire" are rampant.[54]

This is especially seen in Catholic demands for obedience as a so-called virtue, both in monastic/religious life, and in the life of the

50 Ibid., 199; my emphasis.

51 Ibid.; my emphasis.

52 See my discussion of Dvornik in "The Principles of Accommodation and Forgetting in the 21st Century," noted in footnote 19 in this chapter.

53 See my "The Sacrament of Orders Dogmatically Understood" in H. Boersma and M. Levering, eds., *The Oxford Handbook of Sacramental Theology* (Oxford University Press, 2015), 531–44.

54 *Belief after Freud*, 201.

Church more widely with its notions that Catholics are called upon to "accept in Christian obedience decisions of their spiritual shepherds, since they are representatives of Christ as well as teachers and rulers in the Church" (*Lumen Gentium* 38). These are highly dangerous claims, ripe for the sorts of abuse we have been seeing for decades now. In setting bishops and the pope up in this way, the Church runs the very real risk of what Steven Ogden has recently called "epistemic hubris," a fault characteristic of bishops and hierarchs in part because, he says, they still operate under "the spell of monarchy and the sacralization of obedience."

Here, let me be clear: in their capacity to dogmatize, that is, to formally proclaim in a solemn assembly something as creedal and binding — as happened, e.g., at the first two ecumenical councils giving us the creed we still use (Nicaea I and Constantinople I in the fourth century) — the bishops are indeed to be respected as teachers of revealed truth. But beyond that — outside of a Spirit-protected and rarefied atmosphere like an ecumenical council on a major point of dogma — should the utterances of bishops and the pope be given anything at all like reverence (never mind "obedience")? Today, sadly, the answer is plain for all to see: they have squandered whatever authority they might once have had by being abusers and by covering up for abuse for decades. All non-doctrinal pronouncements must therefore be greeted not with reverence but with suspicion because they are almost invariably modeled after mistaken worldly notions of what a subject owes a sovereign. While writing in an Australian Anglican context, much of what Steven Ogden says applies *a fortiori* to the Catholic conception of episcopal and papal power, as when he notes that both Anglicans and Catholics take all these models and ideas of power and obedience not from Christ's submission to His Father but from the secular realm. The Church "still has not cut the head off the king" and thus lives very much in imitation of monarchical patterns of sovereignty, territory, and obedience — a point, as seen above, made also by Dvornik more than sixty years ago, and more recently by Cyril Hovorun's scholarship and my own.[55]

---

55 Steven Ogden, *The Church, Authority, and Foucault: Imagining the Church as an Open Space of Freedom* (Routledge, 2017), 83. For more on dangerous notions of monarchical sovereignty and their corrupting influence on contemporary ecclesiology, see my "Ultramontanism East and West: Nineteenth-Century French Political

For his part, Dominguez-Morano has expanded very considerably on these issues with enormous good sense, recognizing not just theological but psychological problems as well. He notes that in the Catholic Church, especially in relations between seminarians and bishops, priests and bishops, and superiors of religious communities and their members, demands for obedience are made, and frequently offered, by those who are too immature psychologically to avoid the many and serious perils to be found here. Human weakness, which is in no way automatically ameliorated by ordination, is especially pronounced when confronted with positions of power and offers of obedient followers doing one's bidding. It takes exceptionally strong and self-aware individuals, who are vanishingly rare, to resist these temptations — as Christ's encounter with the devil, and the latter's offers of power and obedience, clearly shows.

Let it be plainly said: obedience, in itself, is no virtue, Christian or otherwise. It is highly dangerous to make such claims at least insofar as obedience-submission relations too often mask masochistic or sadistic desires. "The motivations that frequently lead to submissiveness and credulous docility in relation to authority are, in effect, libidinal in character," as Dominguez-Morano has argued.[56] There is no reason to assume that Catholics are exempt from any of these psychodynamics. Indeed, as my three examples above show, there is much evidence that even in 2018, in a crisis as severe as anything the Church has seen, there are plenty of laics, clerics, and bishops happy to imagine themselves as living in obedience to the pope.

Obedience thus understood fails for many reasons, not the least of which is — to use a favorite Jesuit word — a lack of ongoing discernment about the nature of the good and of God's will. The superior's will is taken unquestioningly to represent — or, worse, to be — the will of God automatically and without further qualification or ongoing discernment. This then, he says, "gives birth to the dangerous illusion of a community without subjects in which the group, represented by

---

Conceptions of 'Sovereignty' and Their Influence on Catholic and Orthodox Ecclesiology," *Pro Ecclesia* 24 (2015): 366–89.

56 *Belief after Freud*, 185.

the superior, becomes ideologized and the superior's will is identified with God's will.... The dreadful result . . . is the elevation of infantile submission to the category of a theological virtue."[57]

Instead of being treated as those whose only job is to offer obedience to their superiors, the laics today must begin to see themselves as fully equal to, and standing alongside, the clerics and bishops, not under them; they are not children whose fathers rule over them, but brothers and sisters *together on the same level.* They are an order within the Church, as Nicholas Afanasiev showed so well, and their order only makes sense when it works alongside clerical and episcopal orders: three distinct but equal orders, none of which can exist or make sense without the others. This is important and salutary not only for the welfare of the laics but also for that of the priests and bishops, whose weaknesses and tendencies to fall into sin by abusing those "under" them — whether children, seminarians, or parishioners — are now obvious for all to see. By insisting that they are on the same level, albeit in a different "order," the laics are in fact performing what one might call a work of mercy by closing off the psychological opening which makes abuse possible in the first place as clerics imagine the laics on a lesser, lower level. In other words, the laics, by taking their place in the synods and assemblies of governance in the Church alongside priests and bishops, are acting as "brother's keeper" to these latter two, watching out for, and in fact closing off in advance, the temptations of unchecked power — "clericalism" of the worst sort.

This equal-but-different order of the laics and their responsibility for the welfare of the priests and bishops — and vice-versa — needs to be given concrete expression at the level of the parish and diocese. One of the great insights Christianity gave to the world was the fact that human weakness caused by original sin is universal,[58] and the need for humans to build mechanisms to protect each other from those weaknesses and sins is an imperative. We need to hold each other accountable, and to trust no one person, no one group, with a

---

57 *Belief after Freud,* 202.
58 The *Catechism of the Catholic Church* uses "universal" and its cognates many times in describing original sin, esp. in nos. 401 and 402.

monopoly on power, for such monopolies *always* lead to disaster *every* time they exist in *any* context.

We need not invent from scratch the necessary safeguards against the temptations to abuse power caused by universal human sinfulness. Rather, this book is based on the assumption of the ongoing vitality of past models for all orders (laics, clerics, bishops) to work harmoniously in parishes and dioceses in mutual submission to Christ. In doing so, all are responsible for maintaining the Church as an "open space of freedom."[59]

Obedience, then, is not to be abandoned, for in doing so one runs other equally severe risks of narcissistic tyranny and widespread anarchy. Obedience to norms necessary for the common good remains vital, and nothing said here should in any way be construed as undermining that in the least. But obedience in the Church must be reconfigured as having much more open, concrete, communal processes in place first, and only once those are satisfied can obedience be expected.

Authority within the Church is here to stay, and necessarily so. So mine is not a simplistic call to overthrow all ecclesial authority and every office within the Church. Rather, as noted, it is a call to reconfigure obedience as a much more open, communal process in which people *together* discern how to make themselves radically available to the gospel's demands. As Dominguez-Morano puts it, obedience must be seen and practiced as "a way of jointly discerning God's will,"[60] a process which

> requires an encounter and a dialogue between the individual and the superior. That dialogue . . . should never lose sight of the fact that it is inscribed in the assumption of a radical equality, regardless of the different functions inside the community; a dialogue of brothers who are sincerely searching for God's will as something that eludes both initially. Obedience, from this point of view . . . is *a vow in duo*.[61]

59 Steven Ogden, *The Church, Authority, and Freedom*, 162.
60 Ibid.
61 Ibid., 204.

But the duo is not engaged in a private affair. Rather, they are situated in the context of the entire Christian community we call the Church. Thus obedience is a "service to the group, with an open availability also to suspend his own judgment in the course of the dialogue with the other." This is an important and overlooked point: the superior must be open to recognizing his or her own limitations, blind spots, and defense mechanisms. He or she must not have great self-confidence in his or her powers of perception. All superiors — abbesses of convents, rectors of seminaries, bishops of dioceses, and popes — must have a humble openness to recognizing what they do not know, and a humble willingness to recognize when they are wrong and when they need to change their mind or rescind a decision. There is neither weakness nor shame in admitting "I do not really know" or "I was wrong." Such admissions, far from undermining confidence, inspire it to be more deeply rooted. For such admissions are pure acts of faith understood here as "permanent, mutual questioning which never reaches a unitary and final response." [62] For to reach such a point would be to arrive at a kind of crude propositional certainty that turns faith into an ideology, thereby utterly destroying it. For faith is faith in another person whom we cannot control.

If such is our relationship to God — trusting faith in one beyond our control — it must also be incarnated in our relationships here on earth governed by ecclesial obedience, which must not do to others what God refuses to do to us. Thus, newly configured, obedience is, as Dominguez-Morano succinctly puts it, "co-action without ever turning into coercion." This is an especially important point because it avoids the twin traps of sadomasochism: of those who long to be dominated — that is, to abandon and avoid their own responsibility — and those who long to dominate. Neither side is permitted its characteristic weakness, and in this way, he says, we can avoid turning obedience into a fetish resulting in "psychic infantilism and a fundamental attack on the radical equality to which we are all called when we enter the Christian community." [63]

---

62 *Belief after Freud*, 76.
63 Ibid., 206.

That radical equality of the Christian community was characteristic, at least in part, of its earliest eras before it became ever more closely allied with, and imitative of, the Roman Empire and later imperial, monarchical, and other secular polities. As Hovorun has recently argued, "the church is not hierarchical in its nature. The hierarchical principle is not even its natural property. It was borrowed from outside the church and remains there as its scaffolding."[64] That does not mean necessarily that it should be abandoned. As he goes on to say, "hierarchy... is useful, *but not sacred*."[65]

That must be our guiding principle in the remainder of this book: what I would call a realistic pragmatism. We make use of hierarchy only to the extent it is useful.[66] But, as we have seen already, it has ceased being useful in most instances and instead has become destructive. In what follows, we do not propose to throw all hierarchical exercises of authority overboard, however much, in justice, wicked hierarchs may deserve it in many individual cases. Rather, we shall right the boat, which is over-heavy with hierarchy, by re-introducing the ballast of the laics at all levels. Only such a reintroduction can keep the ship from capsizing.

How do we do this? We begin in the next chapter by recovering models of shared authority in parishes first and foremost, for these are the places where the overwhelming majority of Catholics the world over live out their faith and experience God in the sacraments. Parishes are uniquely sustained by the laics in more numerous and more concrete ways than diocesan, regional, or universal structures of the Church, and thus parishes can be more directly influenced by

64 *Scaffolds*, 141.

65 Ibid., 143; his emphasis.

66 Too much in the Catholic imaginary sees some kind of intrinsic "ontological" value to ecclesial hierarchy, which I think is a massive mistake. There is of course a longstanding attempt in the Christian imaginary of both East and West — largely due to the dubious influence of Pseudo-Dionysius the Areopagite — to see hierarchy as something not just useful but something supposedly structured after heavenly hierarchical orders, including the angels. But all such attempts to theologize based on Dionysian claims must be regarded as an illusion in the strict Freudian sense and are thus to be resisted. For a recent take on all this, see Ashley Purpura, *God, Hierarchy, and Power: Orthodox Theologies of Authority from Byzantium* (Fordham University Press, 2017).

the laics. Parishes, moreover, are the places where most of the sexual abuse happened, and where offenders were often sent without the laics being told why. In what follows, we propose models to ensure this can never happen again.

CHAPTER 2

Reforming Parish Councils

Introduction

THOUGH, AS NOTED IN THE FIRST CHAPTER, THE UNFOR-
tunate developments in the Catholic imaginary have, since the nineteenth century, led too many Catholics to conceive of "the Church"
too much in abstractly universal and particularly papal terms, for the
majority of people "the Church" quite simply is the parish in most
important respects. This concrete building in a particular place is
where all the major sacraments typically take place, the parish school
is often where children are educated, and the parish was often the only
place most Catholics encountered clergy and theology—until, that is,
the advent of modern mass media, now including social media, made
"encounters" with the papacy such an unhelpful and unnecessary part
of the Catholic imaginary.[1]

The place and preeminence of the parish is likely going to increase
as the Church makes her way slowly through her current crucifixion.
It seems very likely that one of the many effects of the abuse crisis will
be to make many, perhaps most, Catholics de facto congregationalists.
In other words, the operative ecclesiology, if one can call it that, will
be not merely heavily focused on the local parish that congregates
each week for Mass, but will be focused on that body at the cost of
ignoring, and perhaps even isolating and excluding, the bishops and
popes, whose words and actions will be spurned even more than they
have been for several decades. For the bishops, including the bishop

---

1 One recent study looks at parishes and their councils and offers some helpful
data: Craig T. Maier, "Discerning the Signs of the Times in American Catholicism:
Parish Pastoral Councils and Parish Pastoral Research," *Journal of Religious Leadership*
13 (2014): 133–60.

of Rome, have so severely undermined their own standing and claims to any kind of authority to ensure they live for the foreseeable future shrouded in ignominy.

This is in some ways a development to be welcomed. We need such a decentering, a dethroning, of popes and bishops, not only because they have proven so often to be abusers or those who cover up abuse, but also and especially because, as noted earlier, they are in no way entitled to a monopoly on power or to be thought of as immune to the effects of original sin, which so often manifests itself in abuses of power. Thus popes and bishops *should* be shunted from the center of the Catholic imaginary to that place so beloved by the current bishop of Rome—the peripheries. But we must not imagine that our task ends there. It is only beginning.

If Catholics are increasingly ignoring anything episcopal or papal, they will still have to contend with those forces even in sheltered, thriving parishes, for the current canons maintain the monopoly on power over parishes in the hands of bishops and their delegates, the priests. That monopoly, however, is very recently acquired (and it looks increasingly unstable). Many parishes, at their foundation in the nineteenth century—or earlier—were often entirely run by the laics.[2]

The Central Role of the Laics

I DRAW THE TERM LAICS AND ITS UNDERLYING RATIONALE from Nicholas Afanasiev's *The Church of the Holy Spirit*, one of the most important books in ecclesiology to be published in the last century.[3] Afanasiev was an Eastern Orthodox theologian granted the

---

2 Some good history may be found in James A. Coriden, *The Parish in Catholic Tradition: History, Theology and Canon Law* (New York: Paulist Press, 1997).

3 Nicholas Afanasiev, *The Church of the Holy Spirit*, trans. Vitaly Permiakov, ed. Michael Plekon (University of Notre Dame Press, 2007). As Permiakov explains in a note, the term *laics* seems to be a calque of a Russian neologism, *laik*, itself based in Afanasiev's mind on the Greek *laikos*. Afanasiev uses the term *laics* as I shall: to designate an equivalent order or rank to *cleric*. In other words, it is not adequate or accurate to assume that laics = laity if the latter term is taken, as it so is in common usage, to mean a person who is not of a particular "professional" rank or who lacks all background and training—a "non-cleric" in other words. The laics for Afanasiev,

rare privilege of being cited in the documents of, and influential on the debates at, Vatican II. He argued that the laics are an order equal to and standing alongside clergy and bishops, all of them exercising their respective roles in living out the one royal priesthood of Christ into which we are *all* baptized. For Afanasiev, as for me, laics are not "lay" people in the sense so often used to denote non-professionals, or those without an office, training, or relevant responsibilities. Precisely to guard against this common thinking—of lay people as those lacking something or somehow deficient—I shall use Afanasiev's somewhat ungainly laics throughout this book as a reminder of their unique status and order within the Church. For Afanasiev, as for many other Christians, especially in the Anglican Communion and the Armenian Apostolic Church, the laics are an order within the Church and the Church can only function as such when the orders of laics and clergy work together under the eucharistic presidency of the order of bishops. This crucial insight, of impeccable theological orthodoxy and ancient historical provenance, is almost nowhere to be found in the Catholic Church today, and that lack is a very large part of the current crisis. Remedying it will therefore be a very large part of the beginning of the long process of healing.

Laics have their own proper ministry *within* the Church, too, and this is marked by what Afanasiev called their "ordination," which takes place at their baptism-chrismation, the sacramental initiation which all members of Christ's body share in common.[4] Reviewing early manuscript evidence of baptismal rituals, Afanasiev discerns in there a five-fold pattern that matches that of ordination:

---

as for me, are an order in their own right in the Church, a point whose practical consequences I shall develop in several chapters in this book.

4 In the early Church, those separate sacraments as we know them today—baptism, then chrismation (what the West would come to call confirmation), then the Eucharist—were all given together as part of the one ritual of illumination, which was given to infants, children, and adults alike. Only later, for reasons we need not be concerned with here, were they parceled out into separate sacraments, and later still restricted by artificial standards of age and "reason." A good treatment of these complicated questions is found in Nicholas Denysenko, *Chrismation: A Primer for Catholics* (Liturgical Press, 2014).

- Laying on of hands by the bishop
- Being anointed
- Being clothed
- Being tonsured
- Being led around the altar[5]

As a result of this sacramental initiation at episcopal hands, Afanasiev insists very strongly that "according to authentic ecclesial thinking, being a laic means being ordained. . . . That is why a laic cannot be viewed in opposition to the consecrated." A lay person in the Church is, then, a contradiction in terms, for "lay" here means "common" and "worldly" whereas the Church is composed of those taken out of the world and set apart by the outpouring of the Holy Spirit.[6]

Just as that initiation was not, in the early Church, separated into the discrete sacraments we know today as baptism, chrismation, and then eucharist, so too, Afanasiev says, the separation of laics and clerics was largely unknown to the early Church. Later still, that separation became an elevation in which clerics were seen to be above the laics and the latter's job reduced to one of compliant obedience to the former. Such a view is theologically indefensible for "no one in the Church can by his nature stand higher than another, although he can fulfill a ministry that is higher than the ministries of others."[7] In this way, Afanasiev recognizes — as Catholic theology also does — that everyone shares in the royal priesthood of Christ, but clerics do so by also exercising a ministerial or sacramental priesthood.[8]

In this light, Afanasiev's theology is significantly sounder than the notion one often hears from certain Catholic sources which argue that the ministry of the laity is to take the mission of the Church into their daily business in the world, but to leave the actual running of

---

5 Modern West-Roman baptismal ritual has lost some of these elements, but they are preserved in the Byzantine rite.

6 Afanasiev, *The Church of the Holy Spirit,* 31.

7 Ibid., 17.

8 Cf. *Lumen Gentium* no. 10: "the common priesthood of the faithful and the ministerial or hierarchical priesthood are . . . interrelated: each of them in its own special way is a participation in the one priesthood of Christ."

the Church to the clergy, as though these latter were somehow not in the world and the former somehow not really part of, or certainly responsible for, the welfare of the Church.[9] Afanasiev rejects that notion, and so must we all. The reasons are painfully manifest: the clergy have had a monopoly on running the Church, and have brought her to a moment of supreme peril throughout much of the world. Never again can they be trusted with such a monopoly, and never again trusted with unchecked power for the simple reason that *nobody* should *ever* be trusted with unchecked power. It is a profoundly foolish thing to presume that *anybody* can be trusted with such power.

The Church has been unbelievably fatuous in giving such a license to its clergy and in so doing ignoring her own central doctrine of original sin.[10] Anyone who takes seriously the doctrine of original sin — which, as Chesterton famously quipped, is the one part of Christian doctrine that can be empirically proven — knows immediately that it so often manifests itself via *libido dominandi*, for which the present crisis provides myriad examples. The phrase is to be found in Augustine of Hippo's landmark work *City of God* (book III, ch. 14; cf. II.18) and is initially used in looking at pre-Christian Roman imperial behavior and the *lust to dominate* others and a *lust for power* more generally.[11] But nothing in him or the subsequent tradition suggests that Christians are exempt from such lusts, and as we know from just papal, never mind wider ecclesial, history, there are multiple examples down through the ages of popes trying to dominate not merely other bishops, but Eastern patriarchs, English queens, German emperors, Italian princes, and others. Similarly, local bishops and parish clergy have tried to do similar things with their own people.

Trusting *anybody,* including clerics, with a monopoly on power is the height of folly; for fallen human nature is not automatically

9 To which Hugh Lawrence has rightly retorted: "In general the co-responsibility of lay Christians for the mission of the Church necessarily involves their participation in its governance." "Ordination and Governance" in B. Hoose, ed., *Authority in the Roman Catholic Church: Theory and Practice* (Ashgate, 2002), 81. See also his "Spiritual Authority and Governance: An Historical Perspective" in the same volume.

10 See nos. 396–409 of the universal Catechism.

11 I first encountered the phrase more than twenty years ago in John Rist's excellent study, *Augustine: Ancient Thought Baptized* (Cambridge University Press, 1996).

restrained or improved in any way by slapping a Roman collar on a man or even laying hands on his head in sacramental ordination. Ordination in no way automatically makes a man stronger or holier—he must still fight his own weaknesses.[12] To think otherwise is to indulge in the kind of totemic or magical thinking that leaves Christianity completely vulnerable to the critique of its more psychologically aware and culturally learned critics.

Given that the Church pioneered the concept of original sin,[13] which one could almost see as a trademarked or copyrighted phrase, and given her long experience with sinners, and her own equally long and frequent failings and falls into corruption in the past, one would expect that if any organization the world over should have strict safeguards in place to inhibit as far as possible the exercise of unchecked power, it would be the Church. And yet the modern period, from 1800 onward, shows a regression in the Church: in the rush to embrace an omnipotent and centralized papacy, and all that follows from that in establishing comparable monopolies by bishops in their dioceses and priests in their parishes, the Church has retreated from the hard-won sober wisdom of Augustine and foolishly imagined that *libido dominandi* is a disorder found only among unruly Roman generals and emperors outside the Church and never Roman pontiffs or others in the Church. This is equivalent to the directors of the Society for Pulmonary Health lecturing everyone else about the lethal dangers of smoking while themselves burning through six packs a day and magically expecting to stay healthy.

The Church's increasing failure over the last two centuries to be on guard against the temptations of unchecked power have brought

---

12 It is a species of popular piety among some that priests are, we are told, especially hated by the devil and thus subject to even fiercer and more frequent temptations to sin and to abuse their power and their office more generally. If this is true—and recent evidence suggests it is—then clerics should perhaps be trusted *even less* with *any* kind of power other than the strictly sacramental.

13 There is an argument to be made in this as in many other instances that Freud's idea of the death drive is simply his attempt to account for the same reality, the same problems, as the doctrine of original sin attempts to do. For more on this see the very suggestive and learned study of Paul Axton, *The Psychotheology of Sin and Salvation: An Analysis of the Meaning of the Death of Christ in Light of the Psychoanalytical Reading of Paul* (T&T Clark, 2015).

about her present and prolonged chastisement. If we learn nothing else from this protracted agony, it must be that trusting clergy with unchecked power in the Church is a *catastrophic* mistake that can *never* be made again.

The sins committed against children are, to be sure, sexual sins, but — as we should long ago have learned from Augustine, and more recently from Freud — sexual desire is an entanglement of many desires, not least the desires to dominate and/or be dominated.[14] Any attempt to avoid this issue, or to substitute for frank discussions pious platitudes about how we just need to be more faithful, more prayerful, more ascetic, is great foolishness. A refusal to talk about, and then begin to dismantle, the present monopolies on power held by priests, bishops, and popes is a sure sign that people are not serious about change. The old ways of governing the Church must be crucified or there will be no resurrection.

Let us not mistake a forthright discussion about power and its monopoly for thinking that what is proposed here is simply a substitution of one set of monopolizing actors for another — a power-grab by an angry laity, as some are already portraying calls for reform today.[15] The Italian historian Benedetto Croce's reputed warning echoes in my ears here: history, he said, is a stage on which victims and executioners occasionally swap roles. Nothing of the sort is proposed here. What is proposed is not only theologically defensible, but also psychologically more mature and reliable: models of ecclesial governance in which *nobody* has a monopoly but all must share and work *together* in lines of clear *mutual* accountability. Such a model is, in a word, far more *charitable* than the current structures, which are themselves a *skandalon* in the original Pauline sense: something that trips up and tempts to fall into sin the manifestly weak and sinful men called clergy, whose status as such does nothing to immunize them against the enormously seductive charms of unchecked power.

14 In addition to the sources later discussed in the text, see, on this point, the second of the *Three Essays on the Theory of Sexuality,* originally published in 1905 but afterwards updated several times by Freud.

15 As noted above, I am not, under the canons (CCEO 327) a "layman" myself, being considered instead a cleric in minor orders. So it cannot be said I'm advocating for power for myself.

To avoid *anyone* being tripped up by those charms again, the whole Church is now called to new but shared burdens in exercising power. The major changes proposed here can only really have a realistic chance of implementation if laics in sufficient numbers demand them and work towards them. And they must be prepared to do so on a perpetual basis, for these are long-term structural realignments in the life of the Church requiring permanent time, attention, and effort from the laics. These proposals are not short-term and facile fixes.

The laics must now be prepared to play much bigger and more responsible roles on a permanent basis, acting as a permanent order within the Church in tandem with the orders of priests and bishops. If they truly are fed up, and wanting to do something, then the Church needs their hard work, patience, perseverance, and ongoing action and accountability of a truly radical sort. All of us must be prepared for change and for tough slogging ahead.

Note well that word: *radical* means "going to the root" or, as I prefer, "returning to our roots." All the proposals made here are nothing other than going back to earlier practices, well justified in and by the history and theology of the early Church. At the same time, however, I would encourage Catholics not to overlook the extent to which what is proposed here is *already* to some limited extent present in the life of the Church. The changes, then, are not quite such sharp departures from current practice in most instances as they might seem at first blush. For the Latin Church already has, in many places, parish councils assisting informally in parish governance; it already has episcopal conferences partially attempting — under absurd restraints — some of the things synods do freely and fully; and via the ordinariates as well as Pastoral Provision and individual reception of Lutheran and Anglican converts, it already has a handful of married priests.

Whether Catholics wish to extend all these changes across the entire Church, and cement them in place, is of course entirely up to them. It is up to Catholics today to choose whether to crucify past images and practices in the Church and to embrace, here, now, today, the necessary death to the status quo that may, in God's good time, lead us to new life. These proposals, then, are, in a word, going to require *kenosis* of the Church's hierarchs.[16] That is, the way forward requires Christ-like self-emptying of pretensions to power (cf. Phil. 2:1–11) on the part of popes and bishops.

The paradox of kenotic acting, as we know well from Christ but often fail to realize in our own lives, is that its powerlessness contains and releases great power. The Catholic anthropologist Mary Douglas, and more recently the Catholic critical theorist Terry Eagleton, have both realized this.[17] As the former argued more than fifty years ago in her groundbreaking book *Purity and Danger,* "when someone freely embraces the symbols of death, or death itself, . . . a great release of power for good should be expected to follow."[18] If Catholics are praying and fasting in this crisis, then let them direct the most fervent, urgent, and constant prayers, and the most rigorous fasting, to God, beseeching him to change the hearts of hierarchs so that they may realize the necessity of embracing the death of monopolized power structures in the Church. In doing so they will be co-operating with the Spirit in releasing new power for the creation of new life.

Thus we may note that here below kenosis can sometimes emerge when it is not wished nor, initially, willed. It can be encouraged in those upon whom dawns the realization that things will not get better on their own. (In this context, then, and perhaps *only* this context, advocacy of deep prayer and fasting[19] makes profound sense: we must petition the Lord to change the hearts and minds of those intransigently holding

---

16 I addressed this theme in part in my "Kenosis vs. La Bella Figura," *The Canadian Journal of Orthodox Christianity* 2 (2007): 94–106. A fuller treatment may be found in Catherine Clifford, "'Kenosis' and the Path to Communion," *The Jurist* 64 (2004): 21–34.

17 Terry Eagleton, *Radical Sacrifice* (Yale University Press, 2018).

18 *Purity and Danger: An Analysis of Concepts of Pollution and Taboo* (Routledge, 2002), 220. The original was published in 1966.

19 Let nobody think I am in any way downplaying the role of fasting. I have written numerous articles on it for more than fifteen years now in a variety of journals, and at least one of those articles has been reprinted more times in more places than anything else I have written. See, e.g., "Catechesis of Fasting," *Homiletic and Pastoral Review* 104 (February 2004): 6–12. (Reprinted by special request at many Internet sites and in print.) See also "Life in the Fast Lane: How to Fight for the Body While Forgetting about Ourselves," *Touchstone* 18 (March 2005): 24–28. Various other articles on fasting were written around the turn of the last century in several Canadian diocesan papers, both Roman Catholic and Ukrainian Catholic.

onto powerful structures that they surrender those in that same kenotic spirit as Christ surrendered himself to be nailed to a cross. If they do not or will not, then we persist in prayer, nonetheless, especially that of Ps. 109:8–19 on a daily basis.) If enough Catholics, including hierarchs, realize that the present structures cannot carry on as before without being crucified then we have grounds for hope.

Current Practices Historically Understood

ONE OF THE MOST IMPORTANT WAYS IN WHICH THE CHURCH needs to be rebuilt at the local level is by returning to the inclusion of laics in the governing of parishes. Note well what is *not* proposed here: this is not a proposal to allow laics to have the dominance they may have had in some places for short periods of time, especially in the nineteenth century. Rather, the proposal is that the laics work alongside the orders of clerics and bishops so that *nobody* enjoys dominance but *all*—bishop, pastor, and people alike—work together.

Broadly speaking, the history of parish and diocesan structures in this country can be traced as a movement from near-total dominance by lay people in the nineteenth century—the era of so-called *trusteeism*—to the absolutely total dominance by centralized episcopal control today, which is seen most clearly in the canons treating parishes, whose pastor and clergy the bishop alone appoints without any requirement for consultation with anyone in the parish. That monopoly is further manifest in the fact that once a pastor is installed, he has no obligation even to permit the formation of anything like a parish council:

> Can. 536 §1. If the diocesan bishop judges it opportune after he has heard the presbyteral council, a pastoral council is to be established in each parish, over which the pastor presides and in which the Christian faithful, together with those who share in pastoral care by virtue of their office in the parish, assist in fostering pastoral activity.[20]

20 Curiously, the comparable canon (295) in the *Code of Canons of the Eastern Churches* says merely this: "In the parish there are to be appropriate councils dealing

Thus do we see that clerics alone (the bishop and his presbyteral council, that is, council of priests) decide whether it is even "opportune" to have a parish pastoral council in the first place. Let us suppose they do. What authority has it? The next section of the same canon answers that succinctly and not surprisingly: "a pastoral council possesses a consultative vote only and is governed by the norms established by the diocesan bishop."[21] The pastor has the final say in the parish, in exact imitation of the bishop's monopoly on power over the diocese.

The contemporary code is, however, a bit wiser in realizing—as I noted earlier—that even clerics are not immune to certain temptations, including money. As a result, the laics are allowed a role when it comes to money. Thus does canon 537 of the Latin code specify that each parish is to have a "finance council which is governed, in addition to universal law, by norms issued by the diocesan bishop and in which the Christian faithful, selected according to these same norms, are to assist the pastor in the administration of the goods of the parish." This makes sense for at least two reasons: the parish monies are raised by the parishioners; and more laics than clerics have backgrounds in business, finance, and accounting. In addition, if laics are involved in financial administration then clerics making fraudulent use of parish monies is harder to hide. A few recent high-profile thefts from parishes by their pastors in Connecticut,[22] Canada,[23] and elsewhere underscore the necessity of having the laics involved.

There is no compelling theological, much less doctrinal, reason for the pastor to have a monopoly on decision-making in a parish. Such a unilateral monopoly by one person is, theologically analyzed,

---

with pastoral and economic matters, according to the norms of the particular law of its own Church *sui iuris*." I have seen particular norms for individual Eastern Catholic jurisdictions speaking of pastoral councils in exactly the same terms as the canon quoted above: they are purely advisory.

21 Numerous dioceses in North America seem to have published such norms. For two such examples—one American, the other Canadian—see here: http://www. diocesefwsb.org/Data/Accounts/Files/1/ModelStatutesforaParishPastoralCouncil.pdf; or go here: http://rcchurch.com/index.php/policies/parish-pastoral-council-guidelines.

22 https://www.nytimes.com/2007/12/05/nyregion/05priest.html.

23 https://ottawacitizen.com/news/local-news/father-joe-convicted-of-theft-and -fraud-returns-to-serve-catholic-faithful-in-ottawa.

"monotheism" of the most pejorative sort — rule by one "god" (cf. Trent's claim about the priest!). But the God revealed in Jesus Christ is a Trinity of persons who are equal in majesty, with none having a monopoly of power over the other. Church structures at all levels should be icons of the Trinity, and current canons for the structure of parishes and dioceses alike are not Trinitarian.

If the laics can be trusted to work with clerics on a finance council, they can and should be trusted in all other matters, too, excepting, of course, those sacramental matters (and only sacraments) which are the exclusive province of clergy. Yet laics are not trusted even in *non-sacramental* matters precisely because they lack ordination. Canon 129 baldly claims that "those who have received sacred orders are qualified, according to the norm of the prescripts of the law, for the power of governance, which exists in the Church by divine institution and is also called the power of jurisdiction." The power of governance/jurisdiction, ostensibly of "divine institution," is slyly conflated with ordination though there is no necessary connection between them established here or elsewhere. Canon 274 §1 is even more cryptic and ambiguous: "Only clerics can obtain offices for whose exercise the power of orders or the power of ecclesiastical governance is required." Again, no *theological* case is made for these unnamed offices, access to which is again implicitly reserved to those in orders for unspecified reasons. Equally important to note here is the lack of a historical case for this claim, as Hugh Lawrence has demonstrated in several places, noting that the requirement of ordination to exercise governance is a late development (after the ninth century) and completely ignores the fact that many monastic houses were not governed by clerics, but nonetheless had real powers of order and jurisdiction.[24]

The canons do not offer a reason for requiring ordination to exercise power for the simple reason that there is none. No orthodox

---

24 Hugh Lawrence, "Ordination and Governance" in B. Hoose, ed., *Authority in the Roman Catholic Church: Theory and Practice* (Ashgate, 2002), 76–77. See also his "Spiritual Authority and Governance: An Historical Perspective" in the same volume.

theology — ancient or modern, Eastern or Western, whether from the Scriptures or the Fathers — can be brought to support the claim "Church governance is the exclusive domain of clerics." Instead, the best that defenders of the current monopoly can come up with is to gesture vaguely towards such things as "trusteeism"[25] or, if they seem to know a bit more history, the "Investiture Crisis" of the late Middle Ages.[26] But these are not arguments — they are bogeymen.

Were there conflicts? Of course. Were the lay trustees always on the side of the angels? Were the bishops? Of course not. Were the bishops sometimes unjustly shunted aside? No doubt. Were they at times given to acting like imperial overlords? Yes.[27] But the clear case of over-compensation, whereby the Church moved from a dominance of laics determining questions of property and priestly employment, to an episcopal monopoly on those same powers, is merely to substitute one mistake for another.[28] As noted earlier, *nobody* should *ever* in *any* context be trusted with a monopoly on power.

25 "Trusteeism" is a cipher that purports to describe 19th-century North American parish history in which lay involvement in the founding of parishes — often decades before there were any priests, still less bishops, on the scene, for immigration and population growth alike often outran the arrival of clergy — is held up as some kind of period of monstrous oppression and rapacious exploitation of the Church. This multifaceted phenomenon is treated in Patrick W. Carey, *People, Priests, and Prelates: Ecclesiastical Democracy and the Tensions of Trusteeism* (University of Notre Dame Press, 1987). But this model had wide ecumenical application, and many Eastern Catholic parishes founded in the same period were founded, owned, and run by laics. So, too, in the Orthodox world, as Nicholas Ferencz documented in his fascinating study, *American Orthodoxy and Parish Congregationalism* (Gorgias Press, 2006).

26 This is true for much of the second millennium. As Hugh Lawrence notes, "In the language of eleventh-century writers, the cleric was *literatus* while the layman was *idiota*," Id., "Ordination and Governance" in B. Hoose, ed., *Authority in the Roman Catholic Church: Theory and Practice* (Ashgate, 2002), 76.

27 Colin Barr talks about how some Irish Catholic bishops in early American dioceses acted more imperially than the British Empire from whence they came and this resulted in them taking every opportunity to reduce lay involvement in the church to a minimum: "'Imperium in Imperio': Irish Episcopal Imperialism in the Nineteenth Century," *The English Historical Review* 123 (2008): 611–50.

28 This dynamic is illustrated in R. S. Appleby, "From Autonomy to Alienation: Lay Involvement in the Governance of the Local Church," in Stephen J. Pope, ed., *Common Calling: The Laity and Governance of the Catholic Church* (Georgetown University Press, 2004), 87–110.

What is proposed here, then, is a modification of the existing approach that monopolizes power in priestly hands. Not only has that led to the present endless disaster in the Church, but it is also bad theology and flies in the face of the Church as communion of all the baptized united around the Lord's eucharistic table.

Consider, then, that parish councils are not optional extras bishops and priests can privately condescend to erect — or not. They must be a required part of every parish, established permanently whether bishops and priests want them or not. This will require them to be cemented into place via canon law. There are ready-made canons that could easily be adapted and adopted from, e.g., the statutes of the Armenian Church:

> The Parish Assembly shall elect from among its members a Parish Council, consisting of not less than five nor more than fifteen members, who shall be custodians of the properties of the Church and shall, together with the Parish Priest, be in charge of the conduct of the affairs of the Parish.[29]

The parish assembly, in Armenian usage (and often in Anglican, too), meets annually in January or February, and consists of all dues-paying registered members eighteen years and older. This body elects the parish council for a term of two years, renewable up to three consecutive times, with each election being subject to "ratification by the primate and diocesan council" (s. 25). This sensible latter provision ensures that there is some oversight from the wider church in case of local cliques or corruption forming. The term limits also ensure limited continuity after which new blood is infused — though previously elected members can be elected again after a hiatus.

In a Catholic context, what would such councils do, and how would their doing it help avoid future crises? Once again, it bears mentioning that this is not a revival of "trusteeism," because what is proposed here

---

29 Statute 23 of the statutes of the Eastern Diocese of the Armenian Church in the United States: https://armenianchurch.us/wp-content/uploads/2017/04/Diocesan-Bylaws-in-English.pdf.

is *joint* governance involving *both* the council *and* the pastor under the bishop's supervision. No one group, then, has exclusive power of trusteeship. As I have argued earlier, all monopolies of power are always bad ideas and must be broken up. No new monopolies are proposed anywhere in this book.

Thus, very much as in the Armenian Church, a Catholic pastor and Catholic parish council *together* would *jointly* exercise *mutual* responsibility in several major areas. The Armenian statutes[30] provide a succinct list that could be copied by Catholics. Borrowing from them and adapting them to a Catholic context, a parish council would:

> Implement any decisions of the annual parish assembly;
>
> Ensure the auditing of the parish financial statements and send copies to the bishop;
>
> Prepare the annual budget for parish approval, including the budgets of related institutions such as schools or cemeteries; and supervise the dispersion of funds, including those apportioned to the diocese;
>
> Ensure the proper and regular performance of liturgy and other services;
>
> Maintain parish registers of baptisms, marriages, deaths, and other important matters;
>
> Receive, in the event of a pastoral vacancy, a priest sent by the bishop until such time as the parish and bishop together find a permanent pastor;
>
> Carry out tasks assigned by the bishop and diocesan council;
>
> Elect delegates to the diocesan synod.

Thus we may see here that this proposal subsumes the responsibilities of the financial council, as currently mentioned in extant Catholic canon law, into the parish council. The annual budget would have to be approved by the council and pastor alike. All spending above a certain threshold would have to be approved by the signatures of both the chair of the council and the pastor; spending over $10,000 would, as current

---

30 See the enumerated powers in statute 33 at the link shown in footnote 29.

canons already require, necessitate approval of council, pastor, and bishop. If the laics are expected to support a parish with their givings, then they have every right to determine how and where those givings are spent, and to keep an eye on all spending to prevent corruption. Every two years, as parish council members are up for election, parish accounts would first be subjected to outside auditing by a reputable firm selected by the diocese for all its parishes. Those results would then be published on the parish website in advance of elections to parish council.

Second, parish councils would be the place for establishing parish priorities and policies, including for any schools or other facilities (nursing homes, say, or cemeteries) under parish control. This would also include the hiring of personnel to work in both parish and parochial institutions. If some of this work needed to be delegated to sub-committees of the council, or to certain office holders, that would be in keeping with many standard practices today, but all such committees and persons would ultimately be accountable for their hiring and firing to the parish council, which could review and overturn any decisions it felt justified in doing so for documented reasons.

Hiring of the *pastor* would be the third major responsibility of the council, to be exercised jointly with the bishop. This is perhaps its most important responsibility. No more must pastors be appointed or removed on the exclusive say of the bishop. No more can we allow ever again for the situation where bishops can remove priests and send them away in silence rather than telling the parish he is being removed for abuse, or alcoholism, or theft, or some other reason. Never again must the process of selecting or removing pastoral leadership be done solely by a bishop acting in sovereign secrecy.[31]

Throughout much of her history, the Church sought leadership in local communities, which were responsible for raising up such men, training them, and supporting them. The current system, which relies so heavily on outside and distant processes involving seminaries, often hundreds of miles away, is a post-Trent development that has outlived

31 The idea of a sovereign bishop is one I examine briefly in my article "Sovereign Is He Who Destroys the Exceptional," *Catholic World Report*, January 31, 2017, https://tinyurl.com/y8oha6jn.

its usefulness.[32] Local discernment and election of clerics is a practice with a long pedigree in the Church both East and West, and once again Armenian models are helpful here. The Eastern Diocese of the United States, e.g., has in its statutes this:

> A Parish Priest or a candidate for ordination to serve in the Parish shall be elected by the Parish Assembly and his election shall be submitted to the Primate and the Diocesan Council for approval.[33]

In a Catholic context, my proposal is to let parish council and bishop *together* discern, confidentially, the time for a change in pastoral leadership in view of the good of the parish. Let parish council and bishop *together* discern which local men seem to have the skills, maturity, and vocation to become deacons and priests. Let them *together* agree on certain men and seek out the necessary training and formation for them.

Once there is a consensus, then council and bishop together discuss suitable new pastors, interview those candidates, and make a decision on appointing one of them. This is, as just noted, very much the model used in many other Christian traditions of East and West. There is no reason whatsoever that it cannot be used in the Catholic Church.

Thus changes in pastoral leadership must emerge out of a consensus between council and bishop, and only for serious reasons, which do not include the convenience of the bishop or his reputation, and not according to some artificially fixed schedule like six-year terms, and certainly not because a priest feels his career trajectory should see him move from a small rural parish to a massive one in a major metropolis. All such reasons must be frankly discussed in council, and then shared with the wider parish.

What are the advantages of these changes? Why would those who currently have a monopoly on power even begin to consider alternate arrangements? There is, of course, the theology which we have already

---

32 For more on this, see Massimo Faggioli, "Trent's Long Shadow," *Commonweal*, August 23, 2018, https://www.commonwealmagazine.org/trent's-long-shadow.

33 No. 39 of the statutes found here: https://armenianchurch.us/wp-content/uploads/2017/04/Diocesan-Bylaws-in-English.pdf.

discussed, and that should be sufficient. That is to say, this new collaborative model is a much sharper and clearer icon of the Trinity in the structures of parish life — and, beyond them, at all levels of the Church, as the new ITC document so compellingly realizes:

> On different levels and in different forms, as local Churches, regional groupings of local Churches, and the universal Church, synodality involves the exercise of the *sensus fidei* of the *universitas fidelium* (all), the ministry of leadership of the college of Bishops, each one with his presbyterium (some), and the ministry of unity of the Bishop of Rome (one). The dynamic of synodality thus . . . is an icon of the eternal *conspiratio* that is lived within the Trinity.[34]

Beyond compelling theological visions, human beings are also calculated self-actors in some respects, and so it is important to consider the following additional benefits. First, the financial burdens are no longer born by clergy alone, whose education and formation to be parish accountants and bankers is extremely thin. Laics with experience in business and accounting would share some of this burden as members of the parish council. Second, amidst endless reports about shortages of clergy, the changes proposed here would enable those clergy already in parishes to devote more of their time and energies to doing what they *are* trained for: to preach, baptize, to visit the sick and homeless, and to celebrate the other sacraments. In doing so, they could begin to recover something of a healthy fatherhood, whose most important responsibilities are to give life — which is what the sacraments do. (Fathers can sometimes fix toilets or paints walls, but we remember them, and love them much more gratefully for when they gave life to us in higher ways than that — helping us with a problem, hearing our complaints, giving us life-changing advice — but above all, giving us their most precious gift of time, something these proposals would also free up for bishops.) Third, bishops would, by having regular instances of working closely with the laics, have the grace of growing less lonely

---

34 "Synodality in the Life and Mission of the Church," no. 64.

in their jobs, and have fewer burdens to bear on their own, increasing their psychological and spiritual strength precisely by having helpers. They would welcome what Joseph Ratzinger, in 1977 upon becoming a bishop, called *Cooperatores Veritatis*. This was the motto he chose for his episcopal coat of arms, indicating that he did not see himself as sovereign lord over a diocese, but as one who was working with clergy and laics as *co-workers in the truth*.

This model of collaborative leadership in the parish, then, is both right in itself but also offers gifts to priests and bishops, enabling them to shift some burdens they should never have borne exclusively. It allows the entire Church to bear those burdens *together*. This model is also the foundation for moving into the wider Church and reforming diocesan and national councils of governance as we shall see in the next two chapters.

CHAPTER 3

Returning to Regular
Diocesan Synods

Introduction

IF LAICS HAVE BEEN UNJUSTLY EXCLUDED FROM SERIOUS parish governance, then that is even more the case on the diocesan level, where once more we see that very recent modern practice—in violation of a multitude of historical (and ecumenical) examples—is to exclude laics and monopolize power in the hands of the bishop. In doing so, we come to one of the ironies of history: that for all its reputation as a "progressive" and "pastoral" council that popularized the notion of the "people of God" rather than a hierarchical Church, Vatican II actually gave rise to some highly regressive practices in the last half-century, cementing in the clerical monopoly we examined previously. This must change.[1]

Unlike the Council of Trent, which both mandated diocesan synods and was in significant measure implemented by them,[2] Vatican II downgraded the requirement of diocesan synods and other local councils with the result that they have been very rare in the life of the Latin Church, and even when extant, subject to so many straitened regulations as to make them almost useless. In this era of the people of God, their *voices* may have more opportunities—thanks to technology

---

1 After this chapter was written, I read the ITC's new document on synodality, where there are many and very encouraging signs that things might begin to change. In nos. 77–79, there is strong encouragement to revive the institution of the diocesan synod with full lay participation.

2 The celebrated Tridentine reformer, Charles Borromeo of Milan, advanced the council's reforms by holding nearly a dozen synods in his diocese, and a further five in his province.

and social media, inter alia — to be raised unofficially; but officially within the councils of governance of the Church their *votes* are excluded far more systematically than at any point in ecclesial history.

All, however, is not to be blamed on Vatican II.[3] For lurking behind it is of course Vatican I (1869–70) which sealed in place certain claims about universal papal jurisdiction and papal infallibility. But nowhere do we find in its decrees any attempt to justify the universal appointment in secrecy of bishops around the world.

Vatican I was relatively conservative in its declaration, but the implementation of that declaration has not been. A maximalist application and implementation was foisted on the Church in 1917 with the Code of Canon Law promulgated that year. In the modern period, codes of canons are vehicles for implementing the broad, often very general, vision of a council. The 1917 code purports to do this by inventing a claim so staggering it has been called a *coup d'Eglise* by the eminent Catholic historian Eamon Duffy. Duffy is referring to the fact that the 1917 Code of Canon Law smuggled in a new and unprecedented canon claiming that all the bishops in the world were either appointed or at least confirmed by the pope of Rome. Until 1917 no pope had ever attempted such grandiose claims, never imagined so wide a sweep to his powers.

Before 1917, some bishops were chosen by the pope directly, but these were a distinct minority, and it was rare that the pope chose them solely on his own. Normally there was some kind of consultation or at least negotiation with local figures, including various princes and potentates.[4] Normally, too, in many places bishops were elected, and the pope merely informed about it afterwards. They were elected in a variety of ways, but the fact that they were normally elected cannot be disputed.[5]

---

3 To be fair, a handful of places around the world briefly experimented with synods in the immediate aftermath of the council, but after the mid-1980s these too seem to have largely disappeared. For some earlier examples, see Pier Aimone "The Participation of Laypeople in Diocesan Synods Immediately after Vatican II" in A. Meloni and S. Scatena, eds., *Synod and Synodality: Theology, History, Canon Law and Ecumenism in New Context* (Münster: LIT Verlag, 2005), 677–702.

4 For details on papal administration, including elections of bishops within the Italian peninsula, see several of the essays in the fascinating collection edited by Geoffrey Dunn, *The Bishop of Rome in Late Antiquity* (Routledge, 2016).

5 See, e.g., Peter Norton, *Episcopal Elections 250–600: Hierarchy and Popular Will in*

Trent, then, was well aware of and did not dispute this fact, which goes some way to explaining why it so freely insisted, in its twenty-fourth session, that two types of synod were to be held. First, it said that

> provincial councils, wheresoever they have been omitted, shall be renewed . . . at least every third year, either after the octave of the Resurrection of our Lord Jesus Christ, or at some other more convenient time, according to the custom of the province; at which [council] all the bishops and others, who, by right or custom, ought to be present thereat, shall be by all means bound to assemble.[6]

Few if any regions of the Latin Church have held provincial councils for more than a century now—that is, councils for several dioceses grouped together into what is known as a metropolitical province. (E.g., the five Latin dioceses in the civil state of Indiana comprise one province under the metropolitan-archbishop of Indianapolis.) The reasons for this neglect were forthrightly stated by Archbishop Timothy Dolan more than a decade ago when he argued that today American bishops prefer not to gather in councils but to do their work on their own, or in the episcopal conference away from scrutiny.[7]

This, however, flies in the face of the Church's historical practices around the world until the twentieth century. Trent is the norm; Vatican II the aberration. Thus Trent insisted that "diocesan synods also shall be celebrated every year; to which all . . . who . . . ought to attend . . . shall be bound to come." If bishops or others are found to "be negligent in these matters, they shall incur the penalties ratified

---

Late Antiquity (Oxford University Press, 2007) for evidence from the first millennium. For the Middle Ages and modern period, see Joseph O'Callaghan, *Electing Our Bishops: How the Catholic Church Should Choose Its Leaders* (Rowman and Littlefield, 2007). For a study on the gradual move from local election to papal selection, see Katherine Harvey, *Episcopal Appointments in England, c. 1214–1344: From Episcopal Election to Papal Provision* (Routledge, 2016).

6 http://www.documentacatholicaomnia.eu/03d/1545-1545,_Concilium_Tridentinum,_Canons_And_Decrees,_EN.pdf.

7 "The Bishops in Council," *First Things*, April 2005, https://www.firstthings.com/article/2005/04/the-bishops-in-council.

by the sacred canons." Clearly, then, the holding of diocesan and regional synods was taken by Trent with the utmost seriousness.

Contrast all this with the 1983 *Code of Canon Law,* which was an attempt to translate the wishes of Vatican II into canonical norms. The council had little interest in promoting synods so it should not surprise us to read the extremely grudging language in Title III (Chapter 1), covering canons 460–468.

Canon 460 begins by defining terms, noting that a "diocesan synod is a group of selected priests and other members of the Christian faithful of a particular church who offer assistance to the diocesan bishop for the good of the whole diocesan community." This definition makes a synod sound like little more than a slightly expanded gathering of clerics to which laity are reluctantly admitted. The laity are certainly assigned no role in getting the bishop to consider holding a synod in the first place, as canon 461 makes clear: "a diocesan synod is to be celebrated in individual particular churches when circumstances suggest it in the judgment of the diocesan bishop after he has heard the presbyteral council." Thus are the laics entirely cut out of the process of even suggesting that a synod be held. There is, of course, no justification given for this because none is possible. It is a pure monopoly of power and nothing more.

If, in other words, the priests and bishop decide to hold a synod, then they are the major invitees, too, as canons further in this chapter make clear, noting that the bishop should invite auxiliary and other bishops in the diocese as well as vicars general, the cathedral chapter, presbyteral council, seminary rector, and some religious superiors. Only after they are invited is it permitted to invite "lay members of the Christian faithful, even members of institutes of consecrated life, chosen by the pastoral council in a manner and number to be determined by the diocesan bishop or, where this council does not exist, in a manner determined by the diocesan bishop."

If these restrictions on membership and function were not enough, then further and more onerous ones were issued in a little-noticed "Instruction on Diocesan Synods" issued by Rome in 1997, which consists largely in an expanded commentary on the canons reviewed above. It seeks to restrict yet further the freedom of synods, first by insisting that the very questions on the agenda be determined by the bishop alone, and then in the strange requirement that

> the Bishop has the duty to exclude from the synodal discussions theses or positions — as well as proposals submitted to the Synod with the mere intention of transmitting to the Holy See "polls" in their regard — discordant with the perennial doctrine of the Church or the Magisterium or concerning material reserved to Supreme ecclesiastical authority or to other ecclesiastical authorities. (IV.4)

Moreover, while this Instruction allows (grudgingly) for "the opinions of its members [to] be solicited by means of a vote," it adds in the very next sentence that "since the Synod is not a college with decisional capacity, such votes are not intended as a binding majority decision." Even if there is a clear or overwhelming majority view that emerges through such a vote, the bishop is entirely free to ignore it or relativize it: "Concerning the outcome of the synodal votes, the Bishop always remains free to determine what weight is to be attributed to their results" (IV.5). The appendix to this document gets more restrictive and petulant, insisting that "the diocesan Bishop is free to issue norms without a diocesan Synod, since in the context of the diocese, legislative *power* is proper and *exclusive* to him" (my emphasis). In other words: a monopoly once more.

Thus do we see that today's bishop, living in the aftermath of Vatican II and its retrograde canonical legislation, is under no pressure at all (unlike what Trent required) to hold a synod in the first place. He may condescend to consider one if his priests are open to the idea. If he does deign to hold one, his is the only voice that counts before (in determining the questions), during (in establishing rules for how the synod may discuss things), and after: "the only legislator in a diocesan synod is the diocesan bishop; the other members of the synod possess only a consultative vote. Only he signs the synodal declarations and decrees, which can be published by his authority alone" (c. 466).

Canon 466 manifests a justifiable concern to guard against manipulative meddling from outsiders in the life of a diocese, and an equally justifiable concern that the bishop not be bullied into any action he honestly thinks harmful or unwise. It is also in keeping with the typical practice of patriarchal-executive authority in the synods of the Eastern Catholic and other churches. Nevertheless, the canons that precede canon 466 contain certain problems insofar as they reproduce popular but hugely problematic notions of sovereignty from Joseph de Maistre, whose overzealous exaltation of the pope placed him not just at the center of the Catholic imaginary, but claimed he had to be the central figure and authority of the entire world, lest it descend into chaos and bloodshed.[8]

The canons just quoted perfectly encapsulate this idea of the bishop as absolute sovereign in his diocese, reproducing on the diocesan level the same image and idea of the absolute sovereign in whose image the papacy was remodeled at Vatican I. The bishop alone maintains complete control over everything. This is disastrously bad theology leading to catastrophic consequences.

This is further problematic insofar as it ignores the practices of history going back well into the first millennium, when synods regularly involved the participation of non-episcopal members. They ignore the synodal and conciliar practices that govern virtually every other Christian body in the world today, from the Anglican Communion to the Eastern Orthodox churches to the Eastern Catholic churches themselves.[9] They make the Latin Church the most prelate-ridden,

---

8 Thus he claimed that "Christianity rests entirely on the Sovereign Pontiff. Without the Sovereign Pontiff, the whole edifice of Christianity is mined, and awaits no more than . . . to crumble entirely. This sovereign pontiff has virtually no bounds: "the rights of the Sovereign Pontiff and his spiritual supremacy are so sacred in the Catholic Church that they form the very essence of the religion. . . . The Protestants call us papists and they are entirely right"! And more alarming still, Maistre asserted that "If it were permitted to establish degrees of importance among things of divine institution, I would place the hierarchy before dogma, since it is indispensable to the maintenance of the faith." Fortunately, Maistre was given the brush-off by the popes of the nineteenth century, and all theologically literate commentators on his ideas since then have rightly seen them as crazy. All these quotes are in my article "Sovereignty, Politics, and the Church: Joseph de Maistre's Legacy for Catholic and Orthodox Ecclesiology," *Pro Ecclesia* 24 (2015): 366–89.

9 There are also limited examples of something approaching synodal governance in other Protestant traditions, several of which — Baptist, Methodist, Reformed — are treated in various chapters in A. Meloni and S. Scatena, eds., *Synod and Synodality* (Münster: LIT Verlag, 2005).

elitist, hierarchical body on the planet, having almost no serious place for the laics to make their voices and their votes count in any significant way. It is a cliché, but nonetheless accurate here: what we have is not a Church, but an old boy's club. In setting up the governance of the Church in this way, the reformers after Vatican II have contributed significantly to the creation and maintenance of the conditions in which sex abuse and its cover-up could happen. Bishops are plainly under no obligation to consult, much less pay heed to, the voices of the disenfranchised men and women of their dioceses.

By monopolizing power in episcopal hands, these canons mock and undermine the fundamental equality and dignity of all the children of God. It is no wonder that there have been so many and such horrifying abuses of power in the last many decades. The rest of the Church has enabled the weakness and sins of the bishops to flourish by not loving them sternly enough to hold them accountable.

The failure to hold regular synods has allowed bishops to avoid having to face their people on a regular basis. Some bishops respond by saying they are accountable only to the pope, but one of the unintended consequences of an otherwise noble idea—episcopal collegiality—from Vatican II means, in reality, that bishops are very rarely called to account by the popes; for the latter are loathe to interfere too much into the affairs of a diocese lest the delicate balance seemingly struck at Vatican I, and reinforced at Vatican II, be upset too much or too regularly. In addition, there are more than 3000 bishops in the world, and the idea that the pope would or could be "supervising" them all is absurd. No serious organization today generally allows more than a dozen "direct reports," that is, twelve people reporting to one supervisor. Beyond that, supervision becomes so attenuated as to be almost useless.

Such is what we have in practice in the Church today: bishops conveniently claiming to be accountable to the pope, but the popes being generally incapable and unwilling to supervise closely for reasons both practical (insufficient time) and theological (collegiality). Synods would aid in remedying these fatal flaws.[10]

---

10 This is a view that slowly seems to be dawning on a handful of prelates, including Archbishop Charles Scicluna of Malta, who has been a key figure in

What is proposed here is a return to the ancient practices mandated, but not invented, by Trent. What is proposed here is rooted deep in tradition, going back at least to the first ecumenical council of Nicaea in 325, which required synods to be held biannually during Lent and again during the fall harvest. This was, of course, in an era before mass communications and rapid mass transportation. So perhaps a full synodal gathering every six months is not necessary. But an annual one certainly is.

That gathering, we must clearly understand, is to be a real synod, with electoral and legislative powers for *all* members. "Consultative" synods are no synods at all. Synods that have a predominance of clergy are equally bogus.

What would an acceptable model look like? The Anglican Diocese of Huron in which I grew up in southwestern Ontario pioneered a model of synodality in the nineteenth century that was then completely novel, but is today completely normative in most of the Anglican Communion (outside of England until recently).[11] The Huron diocese began to hold annual synods, chaired by the bishop, at which two "houses" or "orders" met, the clergy and the people. The formula has evolved over time, but still approximates the following: every active cleric in

---

the frontlines of Vatican responses to abuse. In an interview in November 2018, he argued that "we bishops need to approach the issue of the sexual abuse of minors together... [via] what Pope Francis is calling 'a synodal approach,' that is we cannot do it alone in our community, we need also to empower the lay people, the laity, in order to help us be good stewards." As he continued later in the interview, "it takes a village to educate a child, and it takes a village to prevent abuse and to approach it properly wherever, unfortunately, it happens." The rest of the interview may be found here: https://www.americamagazine.org/faith/2018/11/23/exclusive-archbishop-scicluna-says-february-meeting-start-global-approach-fighting.

11   There is a long history of synod-like bodies in the Catholic Church in Great Britain. Some historians suggest their origins lie as early as the seventh century under (notably) the Byzantine Greek Theodore who became archbishop of Canterbury and organized the Church into two provinces, each with its own convocation. This was done not long after the well-known Synod of Whitby in 664. See, e.g., E. W. Kemp, "The Origins of the Canterbury Convocation," *The Journal of Ecclesiastical History* 3 (1952): 132–43. Legislation after 1969 has vested the authority of the convocations in the newly constituted General Synod: http://www.legislation.gov.uk/ukcm/1969/2/section/1. For more on this history, see Colin Podmore, "The History and Principles of Synodical Government in the Church of England" in A. Meloni and S. Scatena, eds., *Synod and Synodality* (Münster: LIT Verlag, 2005), 213–36.

the diocese holding a license (what Catholic canon law calls "faculties") from the bishop is a clerical member of a synod. Every parish is thus represented by the clergy attached to it. But every parish is also, on a proportional basis, represented by lay members, usually allowing for one lay member of a synod for every 100 registered parishioners in a parish, though other formulas have been used over the years. The synod meets annually in the spring (though this can and does vary in dioceses) for several days to conduct its business, reviewing progress from the past year, and planning for the future. Debates can range widely on a variety of issues, including debate on the budget for the following year, which the synod must approve.

Between sessions of the synod there is an elected diocesan council, which is much smaller, but again has clergy and laity elected on a proportional basis so that all regions of the diocese are represented. This model—of a larger body meeting less frequently, and a smaller body meeting between sessions of the larger—is extremely ancient, and can be found across the Church both East and West. Even today it exists in the Eastern Catholic and Orthodox Churches as the "permanent" (*endemousa*) synod, which is a smaller body that was historically composed of members living closer to the center of the diocese and thus able to gather more quickly and easily than gathering the full synod from farther afield. This is a model that goes back to at least the fourth century.[12] It was still found in the West even during the infamous Gregorian reforms of the eleventh century, several of which Gregory VII only dared to attempt because his synod backed him up—a pattern commonly found among popes of the first millennium accustomed to synodal governance.[13] He may have been a would-be papal centralizer, but like Pius IX seven centuries later, it not only looked better (and was politically necessary) to have other bishops backing him up, but

---

12 The classic work here is Joseph Hajjar, *Le Synode Permanent (synodos endemousa) dans l'Eglise Byzantine des origins au XIe siècle* (Rome: Pontificium Institutum Orientalium Studiorum, 1962).

13 See, inter alia, Kathleen Cushing, *Reform and the Papacy in the Eleventh Century: Spirituality and Social Change* (Manchester University Press, 2005); and Emmanuel Lanne, "Reazione," in *Il Primato del Successore di Pietro: Atti del simposio teologico* (Città del Vaticano: Libreria Editrice Vaticana, 1998), 213–21. See also the references and discussion in DeVille, *Orthodoxy and the Roman Papacy,* 141–46.

this was the historical practice with abundant theological justification.

Still today, there are remnants of this system in the Roman Church itself. The College of Cardinals, through many twists and turns, has been a "permanent synod" of sorts for the pope, though for a century and more now it has rarely played that role—though Pope John Paul II sometimes called it into session exclusively to give him advice. More recently still, the informal "council of cardinals" used by Pope Francis is a form of synodality at once quite unique and ancient.

Within the contemporary Catholic Church, then, diocesan synods would need to be set up and so, too, a permanent synod or diocesan council. Some formula would need to be found for these elections. Once more, the Armenian Diocese in the Eastern United States has exemplary statutes here which could easily be adapted and adopted. In their canonical documents, they call for the "diocesan assembly" (equivalent to a synod as I am using the term here) to be made up of parish clergy (deacons and priests) and lay delegates elected for a "four-year term" with the term of office of one-quarter of the assembly expiring each year so that every year one-quarter of the assembly is freshly elected.[14] Thus the diocesan assembly or, in our terms here, permanent synod, would include members, laic and clerical, from every parish. In the event that some parishes, as increasingly happens in this era of mergers, balloon into enormous size, dwarfing others, and thus coming numerically to dominate a synod, it would be within the prerogative of the bishop to break up those over-large parishes to ensure that each parish would be of roughly equal size.

For the permanent synod, perhaps if dioceses are broken down into smaller structural units—pastoral regions, say, or vicariates, or deaneries—then a proportional formula could be used of, for example, one lay and one clerical member of the council from each region or deanery. In addition, some means of ensuring that both men and women serve on an equal basis would need to be found.

Laics, then, must be prepared to spend their time in church governance on a regular basis. While the synod would only take a few days

---

14 Nos. 50–52: https://armenianchurch.us/wp-content/uploads/2017/04/Diocesan-Bylaws-in-English.pdf.

of their time on an annual basis, the diocesan council would normally meet once a month or more or less often depending on the nature of business at hand. These are serious meetings having major fiscal and legal responsibilities, not unlike serving on the board of trustees of a university, or the board of directors of a hospital.

There is in the Armenian system, as in some other Orthodox Churches, and across much of the Anglican Communion, a wonderfully deliberate balance between the "one" (bishop) and the "many" (clergy and, especially, laics). If one must use an American idiom, the synod has an intricate and intelligent system of "checks and balances." Better still, and on a higher plane, we can and should see this as theologically superior to anything on offer in the Latin Church (or much of the Catholic Church more broadly, remembering — as noted in the introduction — that the Eastern Catholic Churches have very imperfectly returned to this vision of synodality). That is to say, the synod-bishop model, the model of the many-one, is of course the fullest icon we have in ecclesial structures of the life of the Trinity, the tri-unity of the Godhead where there are three persons sharing one divine nature and one life together in perfect communion. As John Zizioulas has explained:

> The "many" always need the "one" in order to express themselves. This mystery of the "one" and the "many" is deeply rooted in the theology of the Church, in its Christological (the "one" aspect) and pneumatological (the aspect of the "many") nature. Institutionally speaking, this involves a ministry of primacy inherent in all forms of conciliarity.[15]

In very practical ways, this conciliarity is manifest by the bishop as chair of the synod and as the executive authority in the diocese charged with implementation of policies determined by the synod. He also has a veto in select circumstances. A synod cannot meet without the bishop unless it is to elect a new bishop, in which case that session of synod is

---

15 John D. Zizioulas, "The Response of the Orthodox Observer," *One in Christ* 24 (1988): 344. For more on this, see my discussion of him in *Orthodoxy and the Roman Papacy*, 41–43.

chaired by the provincial metropolitan or neighboring diocesan bishop.

Local election of bishops is the other major and necessary feature of synods properly so called that the Church must now recover. The current papal monopoly on episcopal appointments must be set aside as both unhistorical and an unjustifiable violation of the dignity and responsibility of all the baptized who have every right to participate in the selection of bishops. Such elections will, of course, in no way guarantee automatically better bishops. We know from history, and still more recent contemporary examples in such places as the Orthodox Church of America (OCA), that synodal election of bishops can sometimes result in deeply corrupt, or profoundly incompetent men (though in the case of the OCA the synod had the means in place to remove these bishops eventually).[16]

Elections, however, are in no way to be justified or scorned by their would-be outcome: they are justified by the history and theology which recognizes that parish clergy and laics have every right to a voice and *a vote* in determining who their bishop will be. Even Pope Francis, to his credit, recognizes this, as when in December 2017 he openly called for "further study and review of the sensitive question of the election of new Bishops and Eparchs."[17] That was rather cautious, if not begrudging, commentary, but previous popes have been more open to elections by laics and clergy, including for their own papal office. Thus Pope Celestine I (r. 422–32) once said that "the one who is to be head over all should be elected by all. No one should be made a bishop over the unwilling."[18] Many centuries later, Afanasiev, reviewing the evidence of the early Church, would conclude in a similar way: "having been ordained in and for the Church the bishop cannot rule God's people without their participation. Otherwise his ministry of governance would cease being charismatic and ecclesial and would

---

16 I have a case study of OCA structures and responses to a financial and sexual abuse crisis they faced over a decade ago in my forthcoming book *The Future of the Parish in North America* (Cascade, 2019).

17 I looked at this in my article here: https://www.catholicworldreport.com/2017/12/28/pope-francis-diaconal-primacy-and-decentralization-of-the-curia/.

18 Quoted in Joseph O'Callahan, *Electing Our Bishops: How the Catholic Church Should Choose Its Leaders* (Rowman and Littlefield, 2007).

become merely a legal procedure. Legal norms cannot be applied to the Church because the Church is a charismatic organism."[19]

If bishops should not be inflicted upon the unwilling, then synods are the way to keep them further in check once they are elected. Furthermore, the bishop cannot proceed unilaterally in most circumstances if the synod is opposed to him — and the biggest way this opposition can be manifest is via the budget. The bishop can request certain things, but the people must vote him the money and then raise it themselves in the apportionment assigned to each parish — a system also used in the Catholic Church. Synods thus offer a forum for the working out of potential conflicts in annual sessions.

While, as noted above, the canons covering diocesan synods in the 1983 code are condescending, unjustifiably narrow, and resistant to power sharing, that does not mean that local diocesan churches must be hamstrung by them. The Eastern Diocese of the Armenian Church is not restricted. Its canons are admirably clear about episcopal election, saying the diocesan bishop is to be

> elected by secret ballot a) from a slate of three candidates to be presented by the Diocesan Council and confirmed by the Catholicos of All Armenians; b) from the ranks of celibate clergy who are under the jurisdiction of the Catholicos of All Armenians and are at least 35 years of age.

Such election is not a purely local affair — because, of course, no bishop ever exists in isolation since the Church is a communion. Thus, as I would also propose, the local election must receive the "confirmation of His Holiness the Patriarch-Catholicos of All Armenians," which, as noted, is the Armenian equivalent to the pope of Rome.[20] The same requirement should be in place for Catholic episcopal elections as well.

In a Catholic context, changes to the codes of canons can take a long time and require papal intervention; but there is nothing preventing

---

19 Afanasiev, *Church of the Holy Spirit*, 64–65.
20 No. 61D: https://armenianchurch.us/wp-content/uploads/2017/04/Diocesan-Bylaws-in-English.pdf.

an intelligent and kenotic bishop right now, when presented with
evidence of his people's willingness — their eagerness even — to confer
with him regularly, from setting up a synod on an annual basis in his
diocese and pledging himself to follow its wishes. If the laics wish to
see these changes come to pass, then they need to demonstrate that
to bishops now, and to do so in concrete ways, too: volunteering their
time to organize such a synod, raising money to cover its costs, and
then playing their part in running it as well.

If there is opposition to these synods, it cannot be justified ecumenically, historically, or theologically. Rather, opposition will come,
as noted briefly earlier, from what I would call the four bogeymen
of the apocalypse: first, "trusteeism" (discussed above and nowhere
proposed here or remotely on the horizon).

Second, the "Investiture Crisis" of the eleventh and twelfth centuries — a fear revived at the time of the French Revolution and subsequent
Napoleonic interference into the life of the Church in France when the
emperor more or less forced the pope to sack all the French bishops
and unilaterally appoint an entirely new bench, a key moment in the
development of the modern Catholic imaginary whereby it is thought
that such appointments are a papal right.[21] But appeals to that crisis
today are irrelevant and its revival impossible because of both modern
financial systems and also modern secular polities.

Third, "conciliarism" of the fifteenth century; but as with appeals
to the first two, this one fails on many counts and is impossible to
take seriously as a threat when one really understands it.[22] In this
regard, the work of Francis Oakley and Paul Valliere must be read
carefully, for they show that there was no such thing as "conciliarism"

---

21   The canonist John Beal uses similar language to mine here, noting that canon
law on the episcopate and papacy, and the subservience of the laics, comes from a
"baroque 'social imaginary.'" "Something There Is That Doesn't Love a Law: Canon
Law and its Discontents" in M. J. Lacey and F. Oakley, eds., *The Crisis of Authority in
Catholic Modernity* (Oxford University Pres, 2011), 139. He denounces the imaginary
which exalts papal-episcopal power in a variety of terms: "structured inequality"
(144), "benevolent despotism at best" (145), and "paternalistic administration" (148).

22   Only in 2018, in the International Theological Commission's document on
synodality do we find a more nuanced assessment of Constance and conciliarism,
esp. in no. 65.

as some kind of homogenous ideological enemy bent on undoing the papacy. "Conciliarism" was simply an overly convenient name that popes and their votaries gave to any person or idea or movement they did not like because they felt it posed a threat to their increasingly centralized monopoly on power.[23] In this regard, it was no different from political tactics today whereby ideological enemies are labelled and shamed (e.g., "homophobe!" or "racist!") in an attempt to isolate and destroy them, thus saving people the bother of having to engage their claims and refute them with reason and evidence.

Fourth and finally, I have often encountered opposition in the form of rank snobbery. The class-based snobbery which I have heard from clergy and some of my colleagues in the academy runs like this: *sure, we'll accept that history disproves the papal monopoly on episcopal appointments, and we can admit that not all the men appointed by the popes were great; but surely you cannot expect mere* lay people *to be trusted with the task of choosing nominees and then voting for them! Who knows what sorts of dreadful candidates they might come up with!*

This last bogeyman is not just class snobbery, but, I submit, part of a disturbing and increasing contemporary trend one might call "anti-politics."[24] My students, among others, have grown up with this charmingly naive view that the Church is somehow supposed to be above or free from politics. This silly idea renders them virtually incapable of understanding the era of the ecumenical councils of 325–787 when we discuss them in class. In making these claims, and expecting the Church on earth to be transcendentally free of politics and enjoying the harmony and perfection of the eschaton, they are at one with too many contemporary Christians of all traditions. But as I say to my students, there is "politics" in how we have arranged the

---

23 Oakley: *The Conciliarist Tradition: Constitutionalism in the Catholic Church 1300–1870* (Oxford University Press, 2008); Valliere: *Conciliarism: A History of Decision-Making in the Church* (Cambridge University Press, 2012). The latter book is broader than the former, and contains a helpful history of conciliar thought, institutions, and practices across the Western Church before and after the Reformation.

24 For more on this see Paul Fawcett et al., eds., *Anti-Politics, Depoliticization, and Governance* (Oxford University Press, 2017).

chairs in this very classroom if, following Aristotle, we understand "politics" simply to be multiple attempts at asking and answering the question "How ought we to order our life together?"

Today, however, largely I suspect as a result of being too successful and prosperous, and especially of spending too much time on-line, we have lost sight of the messiness and costliness of politics as an *embodied and incarnational* process of people meeting together to argue, to disagree, to thrash things out. It often seems we would prefer instead to be able to sit back in our private domains and shriek at someone on social media, or organize an on-line petition, or co-ordinate how to boycott a company or person whose views we must all stampede to denounce—or to stand about waiting for the pope to fix our problems and send us a new bishop while we do nothing. To all this is added an extra dose of especially Christian snobbery, which disdains the organizing, the meeting, the debating, the arguing of politics as "vulgar spectacle" as though there is any other kind. Politics is supposed to be time-consuming, messy, laborious, and often difficult to achieve change. The Church's political organizing of her life should be no different.

Part of the crucifixion will involve, as argued earlier, a letting go of images and ideas of some pristine past free of such messiness. Part of it will also involve our honest realization that however "messy" the proposals for synods electing bishops are, they are the bare minimum necessary to get us much better outcomes in the form of more thoroughly vetted clergy and lines of mutual accountability between clergy and laics. Surely, by now we have seen unrelenting evidence of bishops who are themselves abusers, and even more evidence of bishops who simply didn't care about victims and who cared only about their own quiet careers not being inconvenienced by "scandal." Surely, by now we are totally disabused of any illusions about a smoothly functioning papal system giving us wonderful bishops free from the grubby demands of local politics and elections.

None of this denies that on occasion in the past in certain times and places "lay" people have been involved in the selection process even to the point of dominating and corrupting it for their own advantage or that of their family and friends. But this must not be allowed to overshadow two things. First, not all lay people were so domineering and corrupt; some of them, in fact, were instrumental in getting such great men as Gregory of Nazianzus and Ambrose of Milan to be made bishops.[25] Second, following Afanasiev, we must consider that cutting the "laity" out of a legitimate role in the Church sometimes resulted in "retaliation in the area of church administration for having been deprived of their priestly status."[26] In other words, by inserting themselves into questions of administration, especially of ecclesial property, offices, and monies, these "lay" people were manifesting what Freud famously called the revenge of the repressed. Their votes in the councils and synods of the Church having been suppressed for no good reason whatsoever, they sought to influence things by less felicitous means.

What I am proposing here is designed to avoid all these problems by bringing the laics back into the instruments of governance in the local church where they can exercise their ministry and order in open transparency and harmonious relationship with the clerics. I am not, however, advocating for *exclusively* local elections. Nor am I necessarily saying that being nominated for bishop of the Diocese of Frostbite Falls requires that one organize a campaign and spend millions running for office. I am merely defending the right of the people of God to order their affairs as they see fit. If they discern that campaigns for the episcopate would be beneficial, then they should not be disdained and prohibited from doing so merely because of snobbery. It is fatuous for such snobs to think that the making of bishops in the current system is free of political campaigning: it *reeks* of politics of the most pathological sort, the costs and consequences of which we are now seeing in men like Theodore McCarrick passed along for years by other bishops, nuncios, and several popes in their hermetically sealed club.

So the proposal here is not for exclusive local election. More than ten years ago, I put forth a proposal that called for synodal elections of bishops with modified papal oversight for the good of the church as a whole. By this I meant that new structures could have the laics and clerics of a diocese elect a bishop from a list of candidates who had previously been vetted by Rome, which could be involved beforehand,

---

25 For these and other details, see the Norton volume referenced in the notes above.
26 Afanasiev, *Church of the Holy Spirit*, 59.

collaborating discreetly with the local nomination committee, so that both could scrutinize the proposed candidates and disallow the nomination of men they find problematic. Thus both Rome and the local nominators would have a check on one another. This would give us the best of both worlds: local information *and* universal perspective. This change recognizes that neither side has perfect vision and both can overlook important factors; but together they are far less likely to do so.

After the list of nominees has been agreed to, then the synod, under the presidency of the metropolitan (another office in the Latin Church that is under-utilized, though I argue in the next chapter for reforms to give it greater prominence) or of the senior bishop in the province, would superintend the election after celebrating the opening Mass petitioning the Holy Spirit.[27] Once elected, the bishop-designate would request communion from the bishop of Rome, an ancient practice still observed today by the Eastern Catholic patriarchs after their election in their own synods.

As noted earlier, these proposals have a long history in Anglicanism and in the Armenian Apostolic Church; but they have a history even closer to home. In the 1990 *Code of Canons of the Eastern Churches*, promulgated by Pope John Paul II, there are provisions (see canons 63–77 and 183–85) for the election not just of a patriarch but also of diocesan bishops. If Eastern Catholics can elect their own bishops, why are Roman Catholics not entrusted with this responsibility?

There is, however, an important qualification to be raised here. As I noted in the introduction, Eastern Catholic practice is far from consistently or perfectly applied. The synodal election of bishops today in, for example, my own Ukrainian Greco-Catholic Church, has two wholly unjustified restrictions, both a result of the deleterious influence of Vatican I in corrupting authentic Eastern practice: the synod elects bishops in and for Ukraine only (those elected for Ukrainian Catholic dioceses in the rest of the world must involve Rome); and the synod as currently constituted contains only bishops who alone have a vote. Neither restriction—especially the geographic one—can be theologically justified.

---

27 Renewed attention to the role of provinces and their regional structures may be found in the 2018 ITC document on synodality at nos. 85–87.

Much more theologically coherent is the practice of the Armenian Apostolic Church, which I have treated in extensive detail elsewhere.[28] As the current Catholicos[29] Aram of Cilicia has put it, the Armenian Church is a "people's church par excellence, a participatory community... particularly in its decision-making processes which give a decisive role to the laity." Armenian laity, as well as parish clergy, participate in elections of everyone from their local bishop to their two patriarchs and two catholoci. The double structures of patriarchs and catholoci are utterly unique within Christianity, and constitute, as numerous commentators have recognized, and as my own studies of them confirm, the ecumenically unique role this church can play in modeling different structures and processes to Catholics and others. The Armenian Church is no longer confined to Armenia, but has parishes around the world. As a global church, then, it has found a mechanism for its global leader, the Catholicos of Etchmiadzin, to be elected by lay and clerical representatives from every diocese around the world. And, as noted earlier, on the local level, laics and clerics also elect their diocesan bishop and national primate.[30] This is a robust and longstanding example of theologically justified local involvement of all the orders at all the levels of the Church. For all these reasons, then, as we look to serious reforms to the Catholic Church and churches (both Eastern and Latin), the Armenian Church remains the paramount model par excellence, which, let us recall in terms of strict Catholic ecclesiology, is a legitimate diocese with legitimate clergy, sacraments, and bishops in apostolic succession. If its structures have much to suggest themselves at the parochial and diocesan levels, what about the national level? To this we turn in the next chapter.

---

28 See my *Orthodoxy and the Roman Papacy*, esp. 107–15 and 205–10.

29 A term virtually unique to the Armenian church and used in a way largely comparable to how Catholics would use the term "pope"; that is, to describe the chief hierarch over not a region but the entire church.

30 Recently updated and available here are the statutes of the Eastern Diocese of the Armenian Church in the United States: https://armenianchurch.us/wp-content/uploads/2017/04/Diocesan-Bylaws-in-English.pdf. Much of the Armenian law tracks very closely the comparable canons and statutes of the Orthodox Church of America, updated in 2018 and available here: https://oca.org/cdn/files/PDF/official/2018-0724-oca-statute-final.pdf.

CHAPTER 4

Reforming Episcopal Conferences

Introduction

IN SOME WAYS, THE CHANGES PROPOSED IN THIS CHAPTER are the logical next steps, on a larger scale, to what was proposed in the previous chapter on diocesan synods. In some ways, moreover, the changes proposed here are the simplest to implement. That is one benefit of having well-established episcopal conferences in most countries today with considerable "infrastructure" behind them. The Catholic Church is clearly familiar, in her canonical and papal documents, with the existence of real synods in the Eastern Catholic Churches so that, conceptually at least, the move from a consultative conference to a legislating synod with electoral powers would not be such a big leap. Indeed, in the first footnote in the 1998 document *Apostolos Suos,* the late Pope John Paul II writes:

> The Oriental Churches headed by Patriarchs and Major Archbishops are governed by their respective Synods of Bishops, endowed with legislative, judicial and, in certain cases, administrative power (cf. Code of Canons of the Eastern Churches, Canons 110 and 152): the present document does not deal with these. Hence no analogy may be drawn between such Synods and Episcopal Conferences.

The firewall that the pope seems to build here between synods and episcopal conferences is correct, but is nonetheless a curious one. It is correct, as I have been pointing out, insofar as synods are *not* the same as conferences, for the former have legislative and electoral powers and the latter has neither. Bishops in synod can do things together if they want; bishops in conferences can talk about things, but rarely act together, and only, as we shall see, under highly restricted circumstances. There is little historical or theological justification for these restrictions.

There is a strong sense in this document that the papacy tolerates synods in the East only insofar as these are the price of admitting Eastern Christians to full communion and keeping them in that state — to say nothing of the ecumenical obligation, as it were, by which Rome has to show a good face to the Orthodox Churches today if unity is ever to be achieved. We shall return to these issues later. But first let us look at the existing structures and what undergirds them.

Current Practice

THE CURRENT EXISTENCE OF EPISCOPAL CONFERENCES IS treated in canons 447 to 459. The opening canon of this section defines episcopal conferences as a "permanent institution" comprising "a group of bishops of some nation or certain territory who jointly exercise certain pastoral functions for the Christian faithful of their territory in order to promote the greater good . . . especially through forms and programs of the apostolate fittingly adapted to the circumstances of time and place." The next canon defines membership in a conference, saying that it "includes those who preside over all the particular churches of the same nation" or, if circumstances require it, of a greater or lesser area than just a nation — a region, in other words (c. 448). Later canons call out membership by category, noting that all diocesan, coadjutor, auxiliary, and other titular bishops in the same territory belong, though only the first two have what c. 454 calls a "deliberative vote," whereas the others may or may not have that depending on the statutes. The boundaries of a conference, whether national or regional, are drawn up by what the code calls "the supreme authority of the Church" whose responsibility it is to "erect, suppress, or alter conferences of bishops, after having heard the bishops concerned" (449).

Structurally, each conference drafts its own statutes for Roman review, and included in them must be provisions for regular plenary meetings of all the bishops (at least once a year, but more often if necessary), and "a permanent council of bishops, a general secretariat of the conference, and also other offices and commissions which . . . help it to achieve its purpose" (c. 451). None of these office-holders, however, have the power to speak on behalf of all the bishops unless all of them have given permission to do so (c. 455 s.4).

Having taken great care to erect a conference and to specify its various offices and members, the conference turns out to have very little power to do anything of substance. Canon 455 says that it "can only issue general decrees in cases where universal law has prescribed it or a special mandate of the Apostolic See has established it." Moreover, those decrees must meet two additional criteria: first, a decree must be passed in a plenary session "by at least a two-thirds vote" of the members with a deliberative vote; and then the decree can only obtain binding force "after having been reviewed by the Apostolic See" (c. 455). The Apostolic See must also be sent a report after each plenary meeting, and anything decided having an international character must be approved by Rome.

The final section of canon 455 contains a curious but revealing additional restriction, noting that where there are no universal decrees having unanimity or special grants of power from Rome, "the competence of each diocesan bishop remains intact." This anxiety about not restricting the diocesan bishop shows up again repeatedly in the 1998 document *Apostolos Suos,* which some commentators see as driven in significant measure by the internal politics of various North and Latin American episcopal conferences, some of whose social teachings in the 1980s and 1990s were represented as veering dangerously close to liberation theology or "Marxism" and other ill-defined bogeymen. Let us turn to that document now.

After giving a potted history of local, regional, and ecumenical councils throughout the Church, *Apostolos Suos* notes — as I did earlier in this book — that councils, mandated by Trent, decreased in frequency over time and into the twentieth century. Nevertheless, it claims, the 1917 *Code of Canon Law* sought to "revitalize so venerable an institution" in canon 281, covering particular councils. Given how few such councils were held anywhere in the world between 1917 and 1983, we cannot judge its revitalization campaign a success. However, it is worth noting that the earlier code "called for provincial Councils to be held at least every twenty years and conferences or assemblies of the Bishops in each province to be held at least every five years, in order to deal with the problems of the Dioceses and prepare for the provincial Council" (no. 3).

What seems to have happened to this vision is that the relatively new institution of episcopal conferences has really taken off, and it has almost entirely eclipsed the idea of provincial councils or other similar gatherings.[1] Part of this may be due to the fact, as the document says, that conferences, "unlike Councils . . . had a stable and permanent character" (no. 4). Accordingly, they became widely used, leading to the Second Vatican Council giving detailed guidelines for them and encouraging their establishment where they did not yet exist.

After the council, conferences seem to have become a bit too popular and influential: while calling them "a most helpful means of strengthening ecclesial communion," *Apostolos Suos* continues in the next breath: "Even so, the growing extent of their activities has raised some questions of a theological and pastoral nature, especially with regard to their relationship to the individual Diocesan Bishops" (no. 6). The wording here is instructive: *who* has raised these questions about the extent of conference activities? And are they legitimate questions worth pursuing? The pope claims that the 1985 so-called synod of bishops in Rome was responsible for raising some of these questions, calling for "a fuller and more profound study of the theological and, consequently, the juridical status of Episcopal Conferences, and above all of the issue of their doctrinal authority" (no. 7). Such a profound study is apparently how *Apostolos Suos* conceives of itself, saying the rest of the document will seek to "set out the basic theological and juridical principles regarding Episcopal Conferences, and to offer the juridical synthesis indispensable for helping to establish a theologically well-grounded and juridically sound praxis for the Conferences" (no. 7). Here follows a tedious and verbatim repetition of Vatican I and II on papal primacy, emphasizing once again that outside of its

---

1 Certainly this is the conclusion of Timothy Dolan's article "The Bishops in Council," cited earlier.

tight restrictions, nothing episcopal conferences do is to be held as magisterial. Moreover, the document drives further wedges into any notion of collective authority, least of all disciplinary authority:

> territorially based exercise of the episcopal ministry never takes on the collegial nature proper to the actions of the order of Bishops as such, which alone holds the supreme power over the whole Church. In fact, the relationship between individual Bishops and the College of Bishops is quite different from their relationship to the bodies set up for the above-mentioned joint exercise of certain pastoral tasks. (no. 12)

The reason for this claim, which reeks of Roman fear of any intervening authority that might outflank the pope, is given in terms familiar to those who followed ecclesiological debates in the 1990s between Cardinals Ratzinger and Kasper, the former insisting on the priority of the universal church, the latter on the priority of the local. Ratzinger's views clearly predominate here:

> the power of the College of Bishops over the whole Church is not the result of the sum of the powers of the individual Bishops over their particular Churches; it is a pre-existing reality in which individual Bishops participate. They have no competence to act over the whole Church except collegially. Only the Roman Pontiff, head of the College, can individually exercise supreme power over the Church. In other words, "episcopal collegiality in the strict and proper sense belongs only to the entire College of Bishops, which as a theological subject is indivisible." (no. 12)

So much of this now seems so abstract and so dated, and is steeped in a kind of extreme individualism characteristic of late modernity — only the individual person of the pope can act; only, occasionally, can the individual bishop do so; but bishops acting together is ruled out of court for no good reason. This document is vague and seems to be aimed at nobody and nothing in particular — at almost phantom debates. Who, pray, is querying the nature of episcopal collegiality or the indivisibility of the episcopal college?

Stranger still, having delivered itself of this little jeremiad, the document then seems to proceed merrily on its way enumerating many things precisely where it warmly encourages bishops to work together, insouciantly ignoring the fact that in all these instances Roman dicasteries usually intervene to do the work over and against the bishops:

> 15. It is not possible to give an exhaustive list of the issues which require such cooperation but it escapes no one that issues which currently call for the joint action of Bishops include the promotion and safeguarding of faith and morals, the translation of liturgical books,[2] the promotion and formation of priestly vocations,[3] the preparation of catechetical aids,[4] the promotion and safeguarding of Catholic universities and other educational centres,[5] the ecumenical task,[6] relations with civil authorities, the defence of human life, of peace, and of human rights,[7] also in order to ensure their protection in civil legislation, the promotion of social justice, the use of the means of social communication,[8] etc.

Bishops are, seemingly without irony, exhorted by Rome to tackle this weighty, lengthy, and non-exhaustive list without getting enmeshed in an "excessively bureaucratic development of offices and commissions operating between plenary sessions." (Only Rome is allowed to do that, as noted below!) The danger here is nothing more or other than loss

2 Except for Rome intervening with, e.g., *Liturgiam Authenticam!*

3 Except for Rome intervening with, e.g., *Pastores Dabo Vobis.*

4 Except for Rome getting a "universal" one published first in 1992.

5 Controversially covered in 1990 by Pope John Paul II's apostolic constitution, *Ex Corde Ecclesia* and, before that, the 1979 constitution, *Sapientia Christiana*, both treating Catholic faculties and universities.

6 Governed by canons in the CIC and the Ecumenical Directory produced by Rome in 1993.

7 Covered by the Roman Pontifical Council for Justice and Peace, which was, in 2016, rolled into the new Dicastery for Promoting Integral Human Development.

8 Governed by Roman bodies and special documents published each year on World Communications Day, a modern invention by Rome.

of control and attempts on the part of "some" of these bureaucrats to undermine the episcopal monopoly on power. This is made explicit in paragraph 23:

> The very nature of the teaching office of Bishops requires that, when they exercise it jointly through the Episcopal Conference, this be done in the plenary assembly. Smaller bodies — the permanent council, a commission or other offices — do not have the authority to carry out acts of authentic magisterium.

There is no reason why "smaller bodies" cannot have "the authority to carry out" various acts. This is precisely how permanent or standing synods operate. Indeed, they can only operate by having the delegated authority of the full synod to meet. So, if such authority can be given to permanent synods in the Eastern Catholic Churches, there is no coherent reason why they cannot be given to comparable bodies in the Latin Church.[9]

Proposed Changes and Their Historical and Theological Justification

QUITE SIMPLY, THE FIRST PLACE TO BEGIN HERE WOULD be for Latin conferences to look at the structures of Eastern synods, not only in the Eastern Catholic Churches, but most especially among the Eastern Orthodox, including the Armenian Church. If we move from a conference structure to that of genuine synodality, then one of the biggest and most important changes — of greatest relevance in the ongoing abuse crisis — will be the disciplinary power of synods.

For all their flaws in an incompletely realized vision of synodality, Eastern Catholic Churches do, nonetheless, have real synods with real powers, albeit, in most cases, powers that have been given a cramped

---

9 The fact that they exist only in the much smaller and insignificant Eastern Churches, and are not allowed in the Latin Church, is perhaps an example of unconscious colonialism at work: it's fine for peasants on the periphery of empire to have quaint customs of consultation and consensus among themselves, but the imperial center has no need of such input for it has centralized all power unto itself.

and unjustified interpretation in order to shoe-horn the synodal tradition into a Latin ecclesiology of papal supremacy. This is clear in
several examples, but see especially the 1990 *Code of Canons of the
Eastern Churches* (CCEO) where, in canon 95, we are told that an
Eastern Catholic patriarch's powers to discipline wayward bishops is
extremely limited: "if they [diocesan bishops] gravely transgress in a
certain matter, after having consulted with the permanent synod unless
there is danger in delay, the patriarch is to warn them; if the warning
does not result in the desired effect, he is to defer the matter to the
Roman Pontiff." There is no justification given for this novelty, for none
is possible. We will return to the problem of discipline presently after
a broader consideration of synodal structures and members.

In the CCEO's treatment of "The Synod of Bishops of a Patriarchal Church,"[10] we find that a synod's membership parallels that of
an episcopal conference: in essence, all sitting or active bishops are
voting members of the synod and required to attend each of its sessions. None can vote by proxy. The patriarch convokes the synod and
presides over it (canon 103).

The question of frequency has a number of answers: the canons say
that the synod shall be convoked: (i) whenever there is pressing business
requiring the consent of the synod; (ii) whenever the patriarch and
the permanent synod (the smaller body that meets between sessions
of the full synod, rather like the executive council or administrative
committee of a conference that meets between plenary sessions) deem
it necessary; (iii) whenever one-third or more of the members ask for

---

10 Elsewhere (see my *Orthodoxy and the Roman Papacy*) I have listed detailed
proposals for the possible creation of regional patriarchates in the Latin Church, not
unlike those suggested decades ago by Joseph Ratzinger and dozens of other prominent Latin theologians, all of whose ideas I carefully reviewed. I will not entertain
here the question of whether the head of each episcopal conference should be styled
a "patriarch" or whether that should be restricted, as I suggested, for trans-national
regional gatherings, typically continentally based. Where, in what follows, the canons
refer to the "patriarch," they are referring to the one who is president of the synod and
its executive authority. In this light, then, and for our purposes here, the president of
an episcopal conference can be seen as performing similar roles as those described as
belonging to the patriarch. Such presidents would, in turn, following the logic of my
Orthodoxy and the Roman Papacy, become inserted into the global ecumenical synod
governing the universal church under the presidency of the Roman pontiff.

it in order to deal with a particular matter; (iv) at whatever times have previously been established, preferably requiring annual meetings.

Synods seek to balance the one and the many. Thus the patriarch or president sets the agenda, but the bishops can modify it if one-third of them agree to do so. The patriarch opens the synod, but requires the consent of the synod to transfer the meeting elsewhere, postpone the session, suspend the synod, or dissolve it.

The synod has, as noted, several tasks. It is legislative: it makes particular laws for the patriarchal church. It is judicial: it functions as a tribunal for the whole Church. It is electoral: it votes for a new patriarch and new bishops. When it decides in any of these areas, it is to communicate the results to Rome and to other patriarchal churches.

The synod is not, however, an administrative body — unless, in particular matters and for a time, it is so designated by the patriarch. Normally the patriarch is the executive of the synod who supervises the implementation of legislation and the general administration of the church (canon 112). He also functions, between synod sessions, as the juridical interpreter of laws when necessary. He, with the synod, draws up particular statutes for the synod and church, and writes rules for various procedures — voting in elections, etc. All these are very similar to the statutes that episcopal conferences draft and then send to Rome for review.

It is, clear, then, that synods and episcopal conferences are similarly envisaged in both the Latin and Eastern codes, though both clearly specify that synods have powers the conferences do not possess. There is no good reason for this double standard — none at all. Throughout most of her history, the Church, both East and West, was governed by synods and local councils. As we saw earlier in this book, the rise of papal centralization and its micro-managing tendencies are scarcely more than a century old; and they have brought with them untold problems and grief offset by almost no redeeming virtues. It is this current system that has brought about the worst of both worlds, with, as American Catholics have seen, bishops here waiting around for Rome to act, and Rome not only showing no inclination to act, but, in fact, as of November 2018, intervening to squelch plans for action put forward by the USCCB.

These current structures have thus allowed bishops to avoid doing things about their brothers even when, apparently, their iniquitous acts were well known for a long time. This was possible because it was felt that any disciplinary actions were only possible by and from Rome. But Rome, for various reasons, has almost never acted, and then usually only under duress and in the most perfunctory manner.

Synods are not permitted such luxuries of indolence. Synods historically allow and, indeed, require that brother bishops keep an eye on one another — and on the patriarch — and air things in the confidential sessions of the synod. Because the synod also functions, as noted above, as a tribunal, it is possible to bring a bishop up on charges and to have him tried in the synod following procedural norms and laws for doing so.[11] If found guilty of serious offenses, the synod can contemplate a variety of punishments, up to and including deposition from office and removal from the episcopal or even clerical state.

Modern Eastern Catholic synods, however, complicate these relatively straightforward procedures. Modern synods are incoherent hybrids, keeping some of this authentic Eastern tradition while also glomming on Latin concepts and papal-centric practices after Vatican I. Thus, in the CCEO, we note in canon 1062 that the full synod is to appoint its own tribunal which is to "judge the contentious cases either of eparchies or of bishops, even titular bishops." This tribunal functions as an appellate court of second instance from diocesan tribunals. Those so judged, whether on first or second instance, can appeal from the patriarchal tribunal to the full synod, and after that in some cases to the Roman Pontiff. But a little earlier, in c. 1060, it is claimed that the "Roman Pontiff himself alone has the right to judge: (1) patriarchs; (2) bishops in penal cases." Later this same canon notes that "other bishops are to be judged in contentious cases by the tribunal designated by the Roman Pontiff with due regard for can. 1066." Thus we see that, as in the Latin canonical tradition and practice, the discipline of bishops in both penal and contentious cases cannot be carried out except by the pope.

---

11 The governing statutes of the Orthodox Church of America envisage just such a judicial process and session; and this has been done on occasion, as I have documented elsewhere.

If authentically Eastern synodal practices, especially of episcopal discipline, are confused by being co-mingled with the modern maximizing and centralizing papacy, then for a clearer picture we look once more to other apostolic and catholic traditions in the Orthodox Churches.[12] In, for example, the Orthodox Church of America, the statutes provide that the admonition of a bishop belongs to the metropolitan, but the actual trial and disciplining of a bishop is the responsibility of the holy synod.[13] Similarly, the synod of bishops of the Greek Orthodox Church in America functions "as a Spiritual Court of First Instance for cases involving Metropolitans and Bishops." Such decisions can be appealed to the Holy Synod of the Ecumenical Patriarchate, whose decision is final. The Ecumenical Patriarchate also has exclusive jurisdiction over any charges which require defrocking of clergy.[14] Similarly, the Antiochian Orthodox Archdiocese of North America entrusts "all matters of hierarchical discipline of bishops of the Archdiocese" to the synod, composed of his brother bishops under the presidency of the metropolitan. It makes provision, however, for overseas appeal to the mother-see of Antioch: "Such a bishop shall have the right to appeal any decision of the Local Synod involving a matter of hierarchical discipline against him, to the Patriarch and Holy Synod of Antioch."[15] The Russian Orthodox Church, currently the largest Orthodox church in the world, entrusts the disciplining, including deposing, of its bishops to its Supreme Ecclesiastical Court composed of other bishops.[16] The final sentence, however, can only be carried out if approved and so ordered by the patriarch of Moscow.

12 One might also look at the careful work done by the US Episcopal Church in laying out procedures for the trial and discipline of bishops, several of which have garnered considerable publicity over the last thirty years. Their process requires a special panel of ten bishops, four priests/deacons, and four lay people. For the relevant canons, see canon 17, s.3 here: https://extranet.generalconvention.org/staff/files/download/15057.

13 See article II, s. 5i, and article XV, s.8, of the statutes here: https://oca.org/cdn/files/PDF/official/2018-0724-oca-statute-final.pdf.

14 Article 9, sections d-f, of the "Official Charter of the Archdiocese," available here: https://www.goarch.org/documents/charter.

15 Article IV, s.2 of the statutes here: http://ww1.antiochian.org/content/article-iv-government.

16 See updated Russian statutes here: https://mospat.ru/en/documents/ustav/ix/.

The pattern we see in these examples, then, is of local synods of bishops disciplining their wayward brothers, with provision made for a final overseas appeal to the patriarchal head of the Church if necessary and if desired. This is precisely the model that should be adopted by Catholic churches around the world whose current episcopal conferences, transformed into synods, would take on this responsibility, leaving the pope of Rome as a final (and deeply historical) court of appeal. The incompetence, indolence, and avoidance we have seen among Roman Catholic bishops in the United States in 2018 would thus come to an end: the bishops *would* have the right and indeed the responsibility to discipline such miscreants as Theodore McCarrick, including removing him from the episcopal order and banishing him to a monastic penitentiary or other equivalent penances to be determined in a penal trial and laid out in law.

In one stroke, then, we cut off the all-too-convenient escape route of bishops and popes alike, as each stands around waiting for the other to act while neither does. Bishops could no longer say it was out of their hands. Popes could say this legitimately now for the initial trial in the court of first instance would in fact not be their responsibility. Popes can remain a final court of appeal, as they do currently for Eastern Catholic bishops and patriarchs, but it is not and should not be the papacy's primary responsibility to judge bishops in the region in the first instance. Rather, the pope is an appellate figure, a court of second instance, which role goes back, according to most accounts, to the Council of Serdica in the 340s. Primary responsibility for initial trial and judgment lies with those closest to the scene, the bishops of the synod. If those bishops are compromised, or must recuse themselves, or if the bishop on trial suspects an attempt to railroad him out of office, then, following the Serdican model, he can appeal to the pope to appoint a different set of bishops from, say, a neighboring region, to conduct the trial, not unlike the move in secular courts to transfer to another jurisdiction if the local scene has been too effectively influenced by media or other factors to make them incapable of rendering an impartial verdict.

In returning to proper synods in the Latin Church,[17] with a much-reduced role for the pope of Rome, we are in fact moving to the pattern and practice that governed the Church in the United States and most others until the nineteenth century. Thus, the last century or so has been an aberration and a period of modern experimentation. It must in no terms be thought the measure of "tradition" in this instance. Papal centralization is not traditional. Roman curial micromanagement is not traditional. Episcopal conferences are not traditional. Synodality is traditional, and it is past time for its full and complete recovery everywhere in the Catholic world.[18] As the International Theological Commission has put it with refreshing directness, "the teaching of Scripture and Tradition show that synodality is an essential dimension of the Church."[19]

17 A move—an extremely slight and generally insignificant move—towards greater synodality was thought by some to be the purpose of the recently promoted changes to the rules for Roman "synods" of bishops, which rules were made public by Pope Francis in September 2018 in his apostolic constitution *Episcopalis Communio*. That document, to interpret it charitably and hopefully, seems inclined to inch towards an eventual synodal model (a consistent and laudable priority in this pontificate from the very beginning), but at this pace none of us will live to see it. These tinkerings do little to alter the "synod" so that it becomes a full and true synod with powers of legislation and election, as the semi-official papal organ *L'Osservatore Romano* has been forced to admit. It is an encouraging start, but does not go nearly far enough.

18 At this point, critics immediately begin pointing to the so-called synods in Rome in 2014 and 2015 that resulted in *Amoris Laetitia*, and the "synod" in Rome in 2018 about which many of the same criticisms have been made by the same critics, who bemoan these gatherings as confusing and full of intrigue. But that should bother us not a whit for two reasons. First, all such gatherings throughout history have been messy and full of intrigue. Perhaps in heaven it is otherwise, but here below politics, ecclesial and otherwise, will forever be messy and convoluted.

Second, we must underscore again that the gatherings in 2014, 2015, and 2018 were not in fact synods. No such gatherings in Rome since 1965 have been real synods for they have had neither legislative nor electoral powers. They are merely consultative bodies established unilaterally by the pope as "international study days of the Catholic bishops," as the late Ukrainian Catholic Metropolitan Maxim Hermaniuk once archly called them. So what critics—not without some justice—complain about the gatherings of 2014, 2015, and 2018 has no relevance *as a criticism of the synodal institution as such*; for those gatherings were *not* synods. For more on this, see my "Short Defense of Authentic Synodality," *Catholic World Report*, December 10, 2018, available here: https://www.catholicworldreport.com/2018/12/10/a-short-defense-of-authentic-synodality/.

19 "Synodality in the Life and Mission of the Church Today," no. 42.

CHAPTER 5

*Married Priests and Bishops?**

Introduction

I WROTE MY FIRST PAPER ON SEXUAL ABUSE IN THE CATH-
olic Church in Canada in 1992, some three years after the horrors of
the Mount Cashel orphanage in Newfoundland made national news
on a regular basis. Mount Cashel, run by Roman Catholic brothers
and priests, contained all the horrors we have come to expect and hear
about later in Australia, Pennsylvania, and elsewhere. It was eventually
closed, investigated by the Church and then by the government in a
royal commission, and its revelations led to large lawsuits and the
resignation of the archbishop of St. John's.

Every time since then, in more than twenty-five years of reading and
writing about this great iniquity in the Church, I find that no sooner
is another story of abuse and cover-up in the news than someone
pops up to say that the solution is to allow priests to get married. My
response to that has always been "No, but . . ."

No: I do not see how it is that men who sexually assault and prey
on young boys and young men will suddenly develop an orienta-
tion towards women and a character capable of sustaining a mature
married relationship to them unto death. As Richard Sipe — who has
studied this problem for more years and in more detail than just about
anybody — has put it bluntly, "Marriage is not a cure for the institutional denial, depravity, and deceit demonstrated by a culture that
has used the 'celibacy' of its clergy as proof of its spiritual authority."[1]

---

* Parts of this chapter originally appeared as "Married Priests: Not So Fast," *Commonweal*, September 6, 2005. I reprint it by kind permission of the editor.

1 "Celibacy Today: Mystery, Myth, and Miasma," *Cross Currents* 57 (2007): 555.

But 1: I do try to meet my interlocutor at least part-way by conceding with some evidence that if, in fact, the priesthood of the Latin Church is opened again to married men — having been so in the past for a good part of its history — the likelihood of these kinds of widespread abuse crises happening again will drop sharply, though not for the reasons commonly assumed.

But 2: Going beyond what I have written before, I would now suggest the Church needs to re-think the ban on married *bishops*. Previously, I have written in defense of a return to a married priesthood, but blithely assumed the retention of a celibate episcopate. Now, however, I think the time is ripe to return to a practice of the early Church — both East and West — which saw married bishops, a reality still preserved today in the Anglican Communion. I say this in view of the number of bishops whose treatment of victims has been a callous injustice in itself. It is little short of staggering to see how invisible the humanity of victims was and is to bishops, who, so often having been processed through the deliberately isolating and cold halls of minor and major seminaries where warm human relationships of any sort are disdained (no "particular friends" allowed!), go on to live such remote, detached lives of great privilege, many of them still having chauffeurs, mansions, and myriad other perks. Their lack of fathering their own children has rendered many of these men less than human in their responses to abuse.

Before going on, let me underscore that this chapter is deliberately last because I think the urgency of this change is considerably lower relative to the other changes in the rest of this book. I also think that this change will bring the greatest number of disruptions and require the most far-reaching alterations to the running of the Church today. Consequently, this chapter is more cautious than the others out of an awareness of the costs — human emotional costs above all — posed by its proposals.

That having been said, there are good reasons to think that opening the priesthood and episcopate to mature men in demonstrably healthy and stable marriages will eventually ensure that the number of homosexually-oriented men feigning chastity will diminish sharply. It will also bring into those offices men who have been, as it were, "humanized" by marriage and children, both of which provide far more frequent—that is, daily—ascetical opportunities for self-denial than the privileged life of a supposedly celibate elite who are not exposed to the daily demands of raising children, which, when done properly, strips a man of self-centeredness faster than just about anything, offering him far more opportunities for mortification than rattling off a few rosaries.[2]

I have never forgotten, and often quoted, a homily heard at the nuptial Mass of dear friends in Ottawa, Canada in the fall of 1997. This young priest, a member of the then-new community of the Companions of the Cross, noted that people were often inclined to feel sorry for him and the "sacrifice" of celibacy. But turning to my friends, he noted (in what was prescient, for they went on to have a large family on a small budget, and one of their daughters died at birth) that the opportunities for suffering and sacrifice in the lives of parents far outstripped anything he would experience. With a candor and self-awareness I have never since encountered in a celibate priest, he recounted that his life is very easy: after a day's work in the parish, he said, he goes home, turns off the phone, pours himself a scotch, and watches a football game or does something similarly relaxing before turning in for a solid night's rest. Parents, he noted, rarely can do that, for they are often summoned to take a violently ill child to the emergency department at 3 a.m., or are lying awake, wondering how they will pay for school fees or anxiously talking about how they can help their oldest child grappling with drugs. By contrast, celibates lead very comfortably bourgeois lives, having not only a salary but housing, transportation, and often cooking and housekeeping provided free of charge. They have none of the gut-wrenching worries that parents of children do, and no talk about priests being "spiritual fathers" will ever replicate the depth of anxiety and love parents have for their children.

Let us therefore abandon, for all times and places, the often misty-eyed pseudo-monastic and ascetic nonsense which, developing from the fourth century onward and rising and falling ever after that, disdains sex and relationships to give people excuses to escape

---

2 The contemporary Greek Orthodox saint Iakovos of Evia has said that "for married people, your prayer ropes and prostrations are your children" and one must attend to them now and not set them aside while chasing vainglorious expectations of piety.

into "deserts" and cells of whatever type where they may indulge their narcissism unhindered by those bothersome creatures known as "other people." Sartre was wrong when he said that hell is other people. Hell is where one is alone to indulge one's desires nonstop without the interruptions of, the challenges from, or the nuisance represented by, other people. The way to heaven (and to whatever happiness we may be allotted here below) comes through the necessary sacrificial serving of other people, and the greatest such sacrifices for most of us are the ones we are often inclined to overlook if not disdain: the domestic sacrifices of serving our family. Whoever it was who said that come the revolution everybody wants to be on the streets and nobody wants to stay back doing the dishes, was a wise and holy person, indeed.

The presence of women and children in rectories gives clergy the opportunity to see and serve them as human beings, and if—as Paul so wisely saw in his first letter to Timothy—a man cannot manage these humble tasks well, then there is no office in the church, least of all priestly or episcopal ministry, to which he should be entrusted:

> The saying is sure: If any one aspires to the office of bishop, he desires a noble task. Now a bishop must be above reproach, *the husband of one wife*, temperate, sensible, dignified, hospitable, an apt teacher, no drunkard, not violent but gentle, not quarrelsome, and no lover of money. He must manage his own household well, keeping his children submissive and respectful in every way; for if a man does not know how to manage his own household, how can he care for God's church? He must not be a recent convert, or he may be puffed up with conceit and fall into the condemnation of the devil; moreover he must be well thought of by outsiders, or he may fall into reproach and the snare of the devil (my emphasis). (I Tim. 3:1–7)

Compared to this very concrete and detailed list, what are the criteria today for bishops? That they get good grades in seminary, impress the "formators" and psychologists, and give evidence of docility and submission to the rector and bishop. But none of that is as rigorous or long-term as serving one's family well. Long-term familial relationship will reveal all deceptions and disorders far more clearly than a few years in a seminary will. If a man cannot serve his family well and gracefully, then he has no business trying to serve others in a parish or diocese.

By having women and children around on a daily basis, in his own family and in the families of his colleagues in a diocese, a man is less inclined to see them as objects for sexual pleasure, or whining victims to be dispatched as quickly and quietly as possible with as small a check from the hush fund as possible. As the influential Jewish philosopher Emmanuel Levinas has taught, the failure, quite literally, to come face-to-face with the other allows one to deny the other's humanity, and therefore to subject that person to the most beastly treatment, because he is an object, a category or label (usually based on some disdained racial, ethnic, or other tangible difference) and thus an abstraction. Children can of course still be objectified and abused, including by married men, but facing their humanity in his own children on a regular basis makes it harder for bishops, confronted by abuse, to care so little for the basic humanity of other children who are victims. Perhaps the most horrifying aspect of reading the Pennsylvania grand jury report on Catholic sexual abuse in that state is the callousness with which the victims were treated by the bishops—an impression confirmed in other places, not least the victims interviewed in the Netflix documentary *The Keepers*. To childless unmarried men, children and other victims seemed scarcely human and barely visible. The priority was not their healing: the priority was hushing things up under the pretext of "avoiding scandal," a term, I argued elsewhere, subject to gross misrepresentation.[3] Part of this surely comes from these men not having undergone the profoundly transformative experience of fathering real children of their own, and of being regularly humanized—and humbled—by their wives.

One saintly Ukrainian Catholic bishop, the late Isidore Borecky, much beloved in Canada, was wont to say that he had absolute confidence in his married priests because he knew their wives were more to be reckoned

---

3 "How the Bishops Use and Abuse 'Scandal,'" *Catholic World Report*, August 24, 2018, https://www.catholicworldreport.com/2018/08/24/how-the-bishops-use-and -abuse-scandal/.

with than a room of the sternest hierarchs. A wife, he said, is a man's bishop, metropolitan, patriarch, and pope all in one. A wife would keep the priest in line, and daily keep an eye on him, in a way a bishop — often hundreds of miles away — never could. This is so important a role that the Eastern Churches have a unique title for it: presbytera (Greek) or pani matka (Ukrainian) or matushka (Russian). As some commentators have long noted in this crisis of abuse in the Catholic Church, the lack of women has aided and abetted the crisis; their presence could well have helped end some of it sooner, for they would be far less likely to tolerate the practices of merely moving abusers around from one parish to another. Indeed, we have recent and powerful evidence of this with women chancery officials in Buffalo, Minnesota, and elsewhere going public to blow the whistle on bishops covering up abuse.

And yet, apart from secretaries and housekeepers, women are rare in Latin rectories, and never there as wives. Why? Here lies a tale of some complexity.

History of Current Practices

CELIBACY FOR THE PRIESTHOOD GRADUALLY BECAME mandatory in the Latin Church and more widely and effectively enforced during and after the papacy of Gregory VII (r. 1073–85) before later outbreaks of concubinage, corruption, and related issues arose anew, leading to the Council of Trent having to further crack down. But celibacy for the episcopate had been widely expected and enforced not just in the Latin Church but in the Eastern churches long before the turn of the second millennium. (The one exception to this rule is that of the Anglican Communion, whose bishops are married.) Why did East and West restrict the episcopate to celibate men, especially when both East and West freely acknowledge that the first apostles and later prominent bishops (e.g., St. Gregory of Nyssa) were married, as Paul's first letter to Timothy plainly recognized?

There are several answers to the question of how celibacy came to be central and required. Numerous historians — Eamon Duffy, E. C. Cage, Helen Parish, Michael Frassetto, and Maroula Perisanidi among them — have shown that many factors seem connected to what could be called "success." As Christianity grew and spread, especially after its legalization under Constantine, being a leader would often prove to be lucrative as bishops and clergy had regular sources of and access to money and property as well as prominent positions within society. This increasing popularity of the faith led, as we know, to the rise of monasticism, as certain Christians felt the demands of the faith were being diluted and diminished in direct proportion to its increasing popularity. And so, in search of a "purer" and more rigorous practice of the faith, some fled to deserts, caves, and mountaintops to practice ascetical rigors in celibate and often solitary confinement far from the madding crowd. Other Christians in time fled to these monastics for counsel and psycho-spiritual guidance, thinking their insights superior to what were on offer in the local clergy who, being married, were often thought (and sometimes were) more "worldly." As the eminent historian of early Christianity Peter Brown once put it, the monastic cells of upper Egypt are now seen to have had rather nicely furnished and frequently used consulting rooms.[4]

Insofar as local clergy were thought to be worldly, they were involved in that most mundane of activities, sex. Thus mention must also be made here of an increasing suspicion of sexuality as Christianity moved into the Middle Ages, giving yet more impetus to the desire to restrict sexual activity at least among clergy, who were under direct ecclesial control — much more so than the laics. Here Brown's 1988 classic *The Body and Society: Men, Women, and Sexual Renunciation in Early Christianity*[5] and the more recent work of David Hunter have made us keenly aware of an increasing tendency towards fleeing and openly disdaining sexual and marital relationships among Christians.[6] Here, too, the scholarship of Charles Frazee and Claudia Rapp reveals the changes in prevailing views of bishops as members of the social elites increasingly pressured to prove their holiness by practices of

---

4 Peter Brown, "The Rise and Function of the Holy Man in Late Antiquity," *The Journal of Roman Studies* 61 (1971): 93.

5 Columbia University Press, 1988.

6 See David Hunter, *Marriage and Sexuality in Early Christianity* (Fortress Press, 2018); and his earlier work, *Marriage, Celibacy, and Heresy in Ancient Christianity: The Jovinianist Controversy* (Oxford University Press, 2009).

self-renunciation, including that of renouncing sex—not unlike the phenomenon mentioned often today whereby today's elites are marked by their ascetical efforts in going to the gym,[7] buying organic and "whole foods," and in general being obsessed with sexual etiquette.[8] As Frazee has put it, "a norm was established which called for serious clerics to lead celibate lives in some form of community. The married bishop, priest, or deacon who kept his own household was considered to be less holy, his dedication less firm, than his unmarried confrere."[9]

In time, these social pressures came to be canonically enacted through such mechanisms as, for example, the Quinisext Council of Trullo, which did not attempt to impose celibacy on bishops—as some have thought—so much as legislate in the context of increasing social pressure on bishops and their marriages, which were now to be out of sight as bishops were encouraged not to "cohabit" with their wives after ordination given peculiar social pressure to hide sexual relationships.

By the late Middle Ages, the Western Church began more effectively demanding and imposing celibacy on the priesthood as well. (Though the East resisted such pressures to some degree, it was not totally immune, and restrictions came in here, too.) Reasons for this were often socioeconomic in nature, perhaps most spectacularly during the infamous Investiture Crisis[10] of the eleventh and twelfth centuries, when married men were often easier to politically manipulate if they wanted benefices to support their families. By the end of the eleventh century,

---

7 See, e.g., "The Consumerist Church of Fitness Classes," *The Atlantic Monthly*, https://www.theatlantic.com/health/archive/2017/12/my-body-is-a-temple/547346/. Or "How Fitness Became a Pseudo-Religion," *The New Statesman*, https://www. newstatesman.com/politics/religion/2018/05/how-fitness-became-pseudo-religion.

8 For some earlier data, see M. S. Weinberg and C. J. Williams, "Sexual Embourgeoisment? Social Class and Sexual Activity: 1938–1970," *American Sociological Review* 45 (1980): 33–48.

9 Charles Frazee, "The Origins of Clerical Celibacy in the Western Church," *Church History* 57 (1988): 111.

10 For some primary sources on this conflict, see Brian Tierney, ed., *The Crisis of Church and State: 1050–1300* (University of Toronto Press, 1988). See also Gerd Tellenbach, *Church, State, and Society at the Time of the Investiture Contest*, trans. R. F. Bennett (London: Henderson, 1940). More recent works include Uta-Renate Blumenthal, *The Investiture Controversy: Church and Monarchy from the Ninth to the Twelfth Century* (University of Pennsylvania Press, 1988).

one influential celibate man, Pope Gregory VII, felt forced to launch what some historians call a revolution bearing his name. The Gregorian Reforms sought to root out corruption, and one potent tool for doing so was the reinforcement by an increasingly centralized papacy of an expectation of celibacy among those already ordained. By so insisting, the pope thought he could regain control over offices and dioceses that in some cases had been the private property of families for generations.[11]

So primarily for reasons of money, property, and political control, then, the Latin Church in the West gradually moved to insist on celibacy among her parish clergy and diocesan bishops. Only later were arguments from asceticism drummed up, a pattern the Church of Rome has used previously when it felt that more nakedly political considerations were too uncouth to admit and more exaltedly "spiritual" justification had to be adduced.[12]

Given this formidable history, the question naturally arises: will not the reintroduction of a married priesthood bring with it the risk of reintroducing these very same problems? The short answer to that is no, for reasons discussed in part in earlier chapters requiring all three "orders" of laic (especially in parish councils), clergy, and bishops to work together supervising income and expenditures. Moreover, we can take some solace in modern financial controls and procedures, not least mandatory reporting to various state governments, which assist the Church in being more open and transparent about finances — to say nothing of canonical controls along the same lines and for the same reasons.

---

11 Whatever benefits of this approach, there were also real costs, as the International Theological Commission finally conceded in 2018: "The Gregorian reform and the struggle for the *libertas ecclesiae* contributed to the affirmation of the Pope's authority as primate. On the one hand, this freed Bishops from subordination to the Emperor, but, on the other hand, if not properly understood, it ran the risk of weakening the identity of local Churches." "Synodality in the Life and Mission of the Church Today," no. 32.

12 See Susan Wessel, *Leo the Great and the Spiritual Rebuilding of a Universal Rome* (Brill, 2008), who shows that Roman apologists only very late began to use arguments from apostolicity to justify Roman primacy. Prior to that, as everyone knew and freely admitted, Rome's pre-eminence had everything to do, until 330, with it being the imperial capital. The same dynamics operate in New Rome — Constantinople — after the imperial capital is transferred there in 330, as Francis Dvornik so memorably showed in his *The Idea of Apostolicity in Byzantium and The Legend of Apostle Andrew* (Fordham University Press, 1963).

Proposed Reform

I HAVE EXTENSIVELY TREATED THE TOPIC OF MARRIED priests elsewhere, and will not repeat here most of that. Let us presuppose, rather, that married priests *are* reintroduced into the Latin Church. That is but a first step, and it would remain an option. Nothing here argues that a married priesthood should be mandatory, for that can create problems of its own (e.g., seminarians, finishing their studies, rush into a marriage before their ordination, only to realize later that they made a disastrous choice of bride).

Going beyond that, I want to treat here an idea I have not advanced before, including in my book on married priesthood.[13] That is to say, I want to propose that the Church reconsider married *bishops* alongside married priests.

Why are bishops forbidden from marrying? The scarcity of documentary evidence makes it difficult to arrive at definitive conclusions here, and we must recognize different practices and regulations in the East as distinct from the West — in some places, ritual purity, in light of the Old Covenant, was important; in other places, a concern for bishops not hoarding property to hand on to their sons was important; and, in other places, other factors played a role. But the broad picture seems relatively clear. From the fourth century onward, as a newly legalized Church began to grow, both East and West — though for different reasons in different places — came to place higher emphasis on celibacy, and as that celibacy was increasingly supported in and practiced by monastic communities, so the Church began to draw from monastics when seeking bishops who were, after Justinian's legislation, now legally required to be celibate.[14]

13 I was prompted to do so by a married priest who is a dear friend of mine: Jason Charron, the pastor of Holy Trinity Ukrainian Catholic parish in Carnegie, PA. He reminded me of mutual friends, also married clergy, who are among the finest priests and human beings either of us knows. In talking about them, we both came to the realization that, but for an ancient rule, they would make superlative bishops.

14 For some of the historical details, see Peter L'Huillier, "Episcopal Celibacy in the Orthodox Tradition," *St Vladimir's Theological Quarterly* 35 (1991): 271–300.

The closer we get to our own day, the more we see that the link between bishops and monastics has been more honored in the breach than its observance, as monastics suitable to become bishops became harder to find. Many celibates who are made bishops—whether in the Eastern Orthodox or Eastern Catholic churches—have never been monastics. (Some candidates, a few days before episcopal consecration, are made an "archimandrite"—roughly the equivalent in the West of an abbot or head of a monastery of men—and take on other monastic appurtenances, but this is a silly charade.) A few of them have been married but were then widowed.

As noted in the introduction, the return to a married presbyterate and episcopate will bring many other changes of considerable cost. Most of those challenges are and will be borne by the wives and children of clerical families, who are often forced to bear those burdens with little to no support for their many costs, which can be very considerable, indeed, as I have seen first-hand among friends, and as has been documented elsewhere.[15]

In the first place, to minimize costs widely understood, note what I am *not* proposing here: it is not a proposal to allow those already ordained, who have vowed life-long celibacy, to get married. There are very solid reasons, long understood by both East and West, as to why marriage must precede ordination, and never follow it. In other words, the model envisaged in my other book and here would see suitably trained men, (i) *after* being *first* married and (ii) stable in their marriage, and (iii) with the permission of their wife and (iv) children, receive the sacrament of orders in the priestly rank. Later some would be eligible for possible election to the episcopate.

This ordering is by design. As I always tell my students: just as you do not want your professor trying to date you—because of the power imbalance, but also because it wreaks havoc on dynamics with the rest of the group—and just as professional associations and codes of conduct forbid doctors from dating patients, or lawyers their clients, so the Church's ancient discipline protects parishioners from a priest on the prowl. Thus, before he is ordained and assigned to a parish,

15 See Irene Galadza's essay in my forthcoming *Married Catholic Priests.*

he would have to have been married for some time. This is what the West even today calls *viri probati,* that is, seasoned or proven men, men of stability whose character and marriages can be seen to be reliable and firmly established. Young bishops, then, would cease to exist. As a general rule, a man would be in his 50s in a stable and long-term marriage in order to be considered for the episcopate. The current expectation of bishops retiring at 75 would be maintained. An episcopacy of a quarter-century is plenty long enough.

Whatever route the West might take to recover a married presbyterate, and through it a married episcopate, it would need to be conscious of several important factors before doing so. A married priesthood should not be thought a panacea to any number of issues — including a so-called vocations shortage. The serious challenges of a married priesthood — administrative, financial, familial, and pastoral — are not to be underestimated.

Supposing, as I do, that this is an important change — but relatively less important than those proposed in the rest of this book — let us turn to the further structural changes that would be required by reintroducing a married episcopate. The biggest change would come in terms of size and would be driven by a concern for the costs (not especially financial so much as psychological and emotional) to priestly and episcopal families.

In the first place, one would have to look at the size of the average diocese, especially (but not exclusively) in the Latin Church today. While nobody denies the need for good stewardship of the resources given by God, the current model is based on the principles governing large corporations, as Joseph O'Callahan has documented.[16] It is never a good idea for the Church to model herself on imperial, national, financial, or capitalist institutions. The Church is called to transcend all those, and to be a sacrament of communion. But such is impossible when the average Latin bishop today heads a diocese whose number of people (employees, priests, laics) mimics and often dwarfs that of major corporations. This is totally unacceptable if bishops are ever to recover any serious practice of being pastors to their pastors, never

16 O'Callahan, *Electing Our Bishops.*

mind the rest of their people. This is also totally unacceptable because the size allows — as noted earlier — for bishops scarcely to know on a human level many of the people they are responsible for; and as we have seen in the sex abuse crisis, the failure to acknowledge the humanity of the victims is one of the most shocking and deplorable aspects of episcopal callousness.

Modern capitalist corporations specialize in consolidation and mergers to increase their size and market share, and often to acquire quasi-monopolistic status, crowding out small and independent businesses.[17] The Catholic Church — and here I really do mean the Latin Church alone — has been following this practice of consolidations and mergers for some time now, as it responds to demographic shifts which are, it bears mentioning, often driven by economic changes, including not least the closing of factories in one place to merge them or open them in another where the costs of production are cheaper. So-called free trade and globalization have had deleterious effects not just on local communities, but on local churches in those communities as well.[18] So the Latin church has been closing schools, merging parishes, selling some buildings, downgrading independent parishes into parish clusters or "regional ministries" having fewer liturgies and programs and sharing clergy with several other communities.

Such consolidations and closings have not, however, significantly altered the size of most dioceses. Nor is the bishop's workload reduced, but instead is often judged on the basis of today's human-resources manuals, or accounting classes, or clinical-pastoral care "modalities" — on the basis of his "metrics," in other words.[19] He is not, in other words,

---

17 For more on this see the last chapter of Carlos Dominguez-Murano's new book *Belief after Freud*, discussed in my first chapter. See also two very important works: Todd McGowan, *Enjoying What We Don't Have: The Political Project of Psychoanalysis* (University of Nebraska Press, 2013) and Benjamin Fong's fascinating book, *Death and Mastery: Psychoanalytic Drive Theory and the Subject of Late Capitalism* (Columbia University Press, 2018).

For application to ecclesial contexts, see Bruce Rogers-Vaughn's *Caring for Souls in a Neoliberal Age* (Palgrave Macmillan, 2016).

18 For more on this see Michael Plekon, *The Church Has Left the Building: Faith, Parish, and Ministry in the 21st Century* (Cascade, 2016). I have a chapter in the book.

19 See Stefan Collini's fascinating article on our fetish for numbers in evaluating people, "Kept Alive for Thirty Days," *London Review of Books* 40 (8 November 2018): 35–38.

judged on the domestic and marital standards St. Paul outlined earlier. And that is a real problem. Instead of husbands and fathers who
happen to be bishops, we have ecclesial bureaucrats, company men
concerned with protecting the "brand" ("avoid scandal!") and bottom
line. As my uncle by marriage, a priest in the Archdiocese of New York
since 1962 put it of Cardinal Spellman who ordained him, "One meets
the cardinal-archbishop of New York. One never meets the man." He
also said this of almost all Spellman's successors.

That bloodless dehumanized approach to episcopal leadership would
begin to change if married men were made bishops. For such a school
of sacrifice as the family surely is would become the real place of testing
and discernment to see whether a man was qualified to accept election
as a bishop. The family plays a crucial role in challenging and checking
careerism from taking hold in a man who wants to spend more time
chasing a mitre than a ball with his son in the backyard. Recall once
more the biblical standard as noted in Paul's letter to Timothy, where the
overwhelming focus is on what we might call "domestic affairs." Thus,
in discerning which married priests would be suitable for election as
bishops, the family should be consulted in a discreet way by the nominators to determine whether the priest meets this Pauline standard or not.

Supposing he does, the family should next be consulted on whether
they are prepared to bear this burden at this time. In most cases, it
would be generally advisable for more seasoned and senior men, whose
children are at least teenagers if not older, to consider episcopal election
because of the amount of time the bishop is liable to be away from
home traveling throughout his diocese. If current canons generally
specify that a man must be 35 or 40 before being considered for the
episcopacy, it would be easy to alter this upwards, specifying a man
must be at least 55, and that his children must all be 15 years and older.

The travel and workload of a bishop must also be examined if the
Church is serious about advancing married men to the episcopate.
The chief examination here must be the size and corporate culture of
most dioceses. By that I mean that we would need seriously to consider
the reduction in size of most dioceses in the Church throughout the
world; for most dioceses, if not always geographically vast (though
many are), nonetheless can be demographically huge, comprising tens

and sometimes hundreds of thousands of Catholics, and in some cases (Milan, Mexico City, Manilla, Los Angeles, inter alia) millions of faithful. These dioceses have corresponding budgets in the tens of millions of dollars, making them bigger than some corporations. That is far too big a burden for a man with a family to be expected to bear if he is to serve his family first and foremost, as he must. A man who sacrifices his family to serve a vast institution like his diocese is a man unworthy of *any* office in the Church, for he has sacrificed not just his humanity but that of vulnerable others for whom he is most immediately accountable before God. To so give himself over to service to an institution over his family is thereby to degrade the Church and his family alike.

If, however, dioceses were much smaller, then the sacrifices would be likewise. They would be more manageable. In the early Church, before Christianity grew so popular and spread so widely, it was customary in many places to have the practice of one bishop to one "city," though city then was of course much smaller and more closely circumscribed than it is today. That is a model that bears re-examination today.

It also raises some important questions: how big would a city have to be? How far from the next nearest city of comparable size? How many additional dioceses would be created as a result? This latter question is likely to be a real point of contention for many who, having been so long influenced by the "bigger is better" model of monopolistic capitalism, think the same applies in the Church. But it does not and should not. Smaller is to be preferred if we are ever to recover any notion (with due caution for all that Dominguez-Morano said about this as we saw earlier) of the bishop as "spiritual father" to his clergy and people. A father needs to have the ability to relate on a regular basis to the people of his diocese. And that means the diocese must be small, or, if that proves impossible, the diocese must be subdivided into smaller units and governed by more than one bishop, making use of the ancient office of, for example, chorbishop, a figure that seems to have been a "country bishop" under the supervision of the metropolitan in the metropolis or major urban center.[20] Though not ideal, the use of auxiliary bishops

---

20 For more on these, see K. R. O'Brien, "Antiochene Maronite Chorbishops in the Catholic Church," *Studia Canonica* 22 (1988): 425–30. For a longer study by an eminent

today fulfills some of this same function. In any case, whether under these titles or some other (the Anglican Communion, for instance, often uses "archdeacons" as regional supervisors assisting the bishop in governing a diocese), new and smaller structural units should be found.

But how small? Merely reducing dioceses to "one bishop in one city" as the old practice had it fails to contend, in the twenty-first century, with something Christians of the first several centuries did not have: the modern metropolis, with tens of millions of people living in the city proper and millions more in the surrounding region. Given such demographic facts, it makes little sense to say "one bishop to one city" if that city is Mexico City, Los Angeles, Paris, London, Sydney, Mumbai, Toronto, or some other massive conglomeration of people.

How, then, are we to say what the ideal number should be? Perhaps there are some general guidelines to begin this process. First, any diocese currently large enough to require auxiliary bishops should automatically be divided into smaller units, and those auxiliaries made diocesan bishops of new territories. Second, any diocese where it is impossible, due either to geography or demography, for the bishop to visit all his parishes in one calendar year should be divided. Thus we may arrive at a rough rule of "one visit by one bishop in one year." There would be some flexibility here, allowing a diocese to vary in size from 52 to 104 parishes. The logic here is human: if I am to sustain relationships, then I must see people from time to time, and a visit of once per year seems the bare minimum necessary to sustain a relationship.

This rule of 52–104 would allow a bishop to visit two parishes, and no more, on a given Sunday. If Latin clergy are permitted normally to "binate," that is, to celebrate no more than two Masses on a day, then this rule of diocesan size follows from that. We might call this the "binate-bilocate" rule.

---

canonist and historian, see Johannes Madey, "Chorepiscopi and Periodeutes in the Light of the Canonical Sources of the Syro-Antiochean Church," *Christian Orient* 5 (1984): 167–83. For a recent example in the Maronite Catholic Church in this country, see Susan Klemond, "Maronite Catholic Pastor Ordained Chorbishop on Feast of the Epiphany," *The Catholic Spirit*, January 7, 2015, http://thecatholicspirit.com/featured/now-bishop. The Maronites, in fact, seem to be virtually the only church in the world to keep this office alive.

Such reductions in size, and consequent availability for bishops to be out in the field more with their people, will play a crucial role in the long, slow recovery of any kind of episcopal authority in the aftermath of the unrelenting, unsparing devastation across the whole Church as a result of not just the sexual abuse of minors, seminarians, and adults, but especially its episcopal cover-up. Bishops, perhaps bringing their own families to visit their parishes every calendar year, and meeting their people in synods on an annual (or more frequent) basis, and meeting some of them in parish councils when collaborating on the selection of a new priest, will slowly show themselves to be real fathers and real men — not "princes of the Church" or distant, cold, calculating, and callous CEOs of diocesan corporations — who share a common humanity with all of us, who collaborate with the laics and clerics of the Church in mutual synodality and accountability, mirroring the fundamental equality of all the people of God around the altar of the Lord.

Only on this basis will bishops begin to recover some measure of trustworthiness and credibility. If they continue to resist these changes, then the crucifixion of the Church will not end, and the trial that awaits them before the "awesome tribunal of Christ," as the Byzantine liturgy puts it, should make us all quake in fear of the Lord, who wants to bring new and risen life to His body, the Church, even today. Will we do our part, and will bishops get out of the way to let the people do their part, so that new life can take root abundantly?

A Concluding
Unscientific Postscript

W HAT DO WE DO NOW? WHERE DO WE GO
from here? How do we move forward?

As noted in the introduction, many of the changes
proposed here are for the long haul. They cannot be implemented
overnight or in isolation. They will require work, beginning with the
necessary politicking to organize and push for the changes, and to
set them in motion. When the Church has changed in the past, it has
often been because, in the midst of a huge crisis, the people of God
rose up and demanded it. Do not be put off, therefore, by thinking
"Well, all power is in the hands of the pope and bishops." These men
are politicians who must take account of what the people will and must
demand. If they clearly see that business as usual cannot continue, they
will begin to change. It has always been this way.

So, it is up to the people of God to act, to push forward, here, now,
today, and not to stop pushing until changes are made and cemented
into place. It is clear as of this writing that waiting on Rome to do just
about anything is a waste of time; it is equally clear that hoping for
the bishops in this country or any other to act is also a fool's errand.
The USCCB gathering in November 2018 proved their utter impotence
and their total captivity to the papal-centric imaginary discussed in
my first chapter. That imaginary has robbed the bishops of any way of
thinking of themselves and their roles other than as docile footmen
waiting on the papal throne for permission to act. It is a pathetic
spectacle to behold.

Thus we are left with the ineluctable conclusion: those hoping for
serious change now see that they hope and wait on *themselves* to act.
In the first and most important place, this means the laics; but it could
also, in theory, include, as noted earlier, individual bishops willing,

in a kenotic spirit, to submit to the changes and push them forward in their own diocese as far as possible. They need not wait on Rome, nor on some pathological notion of "collegiality" or "fraternal unity" to act on their own.

But before turning to action, including the actions described here, there is one additional task to be carried out, and thus do we find in our ending is our beginning. What remains for us to do is to consider how it is that we let go of the Catholic imaginary of the past, including any romanticized narratives and idealized images of ecclesial glory. For it is clear that we must let go of all such images in order to forge ahead with reform of the Church, a Church that must emerge and remain humbled of all pretenses to power—papal and otherwise. How do we let go?

The current crucifixion of the Church is already provoking a lot of sober evaluations of the Church. I have been slowly noticing a much stronger willingness on the part of people to speak out and speak out bluntly about their near-complete disillusionment with the Church and, especially, with bishops today. This is to be welcomed and encouraged to run its course to completion.

Having done that, we next need to learn to forget past images of supposed glories, and to deal with the Church as we have it now, not as it once was—or, more likely, as it was once *imagined* to be. We must come to forget all those vain imaginings for, in Freudian terminology, they are illusions.

It will of course be a slow process and not without pain and mourning. It is best to be open about this. Catholics need to learn to forget past idealized images and ideas, and doing so may well provoke a certain wistfulness, nostalgia, and perhaps even (to use a Freudian phrase) mourning and melancholia as we let go of idealized notions of a centralized papacy as some kind of oracle dispensing wisdom and sprinkling saintly bishops around the world. Popes and bishops, too, will need to let go of, and if necessary mourn, whatever powers, prestige, and perks they may have enjoyed in the past. They can fight this, and some doubtless will, but that will in the end only cause them and the Church they purport to love more pain and suffering.

In more concrete terms, we may well also be entering the era in which we have to say goodbye to the infrastructure we have taken for granted. The ongoing payments to settle lawsuits have already bankrupted several dioceses, and we may see several more dioceses go under. Schools and parishes and their property may continue to be sold. Much of Catholic life in its particulars may be gone for good. All such losses inevitably provoke a certain degree of mourning, and, as Freud showed, it is healthier for this to be open and acknowledged lest it descend into melancholia.

But Christians never mourn without hope. As we let go of old ideas and practices in the now-abandoned Catholic imaginary, let us begin to fill a new one with healthy images of laics, clergy, and bishops functioning as brothers and sisters together. Let us move from a pyramidal model of hierarchy, with its emphasis on obedience, authority, and power, to a model of three orders sitting around three sides of a table, the fourth side occupied by the one who is our head, Christ our God.

In this regard, let us follow St. Paul's counsel (Phil. 3:14) of "forgetting what lies behind and straining forward to what lies ahead" in order to "press on toward the goal for the prize of the upward call of God in Christ Jesus." Going forward, Catholics will need to create new narratives, free of the temptations of chosen glory in a past that never truly was.[1] We have to have before us at all times the example of Christ who "forgot" His "equality with God" (Phil. 2:6) and "emptied himself" of His divine glory, but was in the end "highly exalted." We cannot pray for the Church to be exalted again in the Catholic imaginary. We must keep before us a humbled Church in which none rules over others but all the orders — laics, clerics, bishops — submit each to the other in service to the glory of God.

Such submission and such humble service — for those wondering how and where to begin — can and should start in the parish. Volunteer to serve on parish and finance councils if they exist. If they do not, push for them to be erected. Work to find other parishioners who care enough to work for the establishment of these vital channels of shared governance. And then, once established, do not be shy about putting yourself forward to serve on them and to do the work necessary for

---

1 Let us not indulge in the temptation of creating what Vamik Volkan calls a narrative of "chosen glory" that obscures all the problems of the past.

them to succeed in their initial form with a view to their eventual transformation into the fully endowed councils I have outlined here with real and proper powers that cannot be given or withheld by clergy.

Do the same at the diocesan level. Increasingly it seems in this country that bishops are, slowly and painfully, realizing they have no authority and credibility and thus it will be up to the laics to push for diocesan synods and provincial councils where these reforms can begin to take root. Do not be put off by anyone. For you can be confident that yours is a role given by God and part of the very nature of the Church, as the International Theological Commission has recently put it:

> A synodal Church is a Church of participation and co-responsibility. In exercising synodality she is called to give expression to the participation of all, according to each one's calling, with the authority conferred by Christ on the College of Bishops headed by the Pope. Participation is based on the fact that all the faithful are qualified and called to serve each other through the gifts they have all received from the Holy Spirit.[2]

Make it clear, moreover, that the reception of such gifts as shared synodal governance — in the parish, diocese, and region or nation — is a *sine qua non* of finding resurrection on the far side of this ecclesial crucifixion we are all enduring. The details of how people are elected and for how long, and by what mechanism, can and may vary: but the fact that the laics and clerics alike must now take their places in the councils of governance as orders equal to the order of the episcopate, with the same voice and vote, is no longer in doubt.

The only way any of these reforms will come about will be through politics, which should never be gratuitously scorned as grubby and worldly, but as the way in which the Church, like all organizations, answers Aristotle's original question: how ought we to order our life together? Thus the politics we need today consists in part in the order of the laics pushing for change, making views known, calling meetings,

---

2 No. 67 of "Synodality in the Life and Mission of the Church Today."

planning sessions and workshops, fundraising, and relentlessly demanding in every context for popes to change, bishops to change, and parish priests to change, remembering, in Newman's felicitous formula, that "to live is to change, and to be perfect is to have changed often."[3] We want the Church to recover her perfection as the Body of Christ, and for this we must all constantly change, not just through individual repentance, prayer, and fasting, but through major structural changes to ensure we never again live through a crisis such as the present one.

Relentless pressure from the people of God is what has prompted the Church to change in the past, and it can work again in the present. Let none of us be warned off such changes for "it seems good to the Holy Spirit and to us" that they come about now.

---

3 *Essay on the Development of Christian Doctrine*, ch. 1, s.1.

Annotated
Bibliographical Essay

THE FOOTNOTES IN THE TEXT GIVE REFERENCES FOR WORKS directly cited. The following list gives sources that have been in the background as I was writing, or are useful for those desirous of diving deeper into the relevant literature.

Introduction

FOR MY EARLIER WORK RESPONDING TO THE POPE, AND looking at reforms to the papacy, see *Orthodoxy and the Roman Papacy: Ut Unum Sint and the Prospects of East-West Unity* (University of Notre Dame Press, 2011). This book should now be read alongside A.E. Siecienski's splendid study, *The Papacy and the Orthodox: Sources and History of a Debate* (Oxford University Press, 2017).

Yves Congar's book, whose 1950 French original I read long ago, was finally translated into English in 2010: Yves Congar, *True and False Reform in the Church,* trans. Paul Philibert (Liturgical Press). It is a lengthy, careful overview of reforms for which it presents a typology of sorts. Congar is one of the most important theologians of the last century. I would also warmly recommend, for its acerbic humor and blunt assessments, his *Journal of the Council,* trans. M.J. Ronayne and M.C. Boulding (Liturgical Press, 2012).

For more on ecumenical gifts, see the very accessible work of the late Margaret O'Gara, *The Ecumenical Gift Exchange* (Liturgical Press, 1998). O'Gara's book, *Triumph in Defeat: Infallibility, Vatican I, and the French Minority Bishops* (Catholic University of America Press, 1988) remains valuable for understanding this council, though more recent works, noted below, give a more comprehensive view.

For a fascinating collection of essays that attempt to look at what it would require for Catholics to not just receive but learn from and even implement some of the gifts received from other Christian traditions, see P. Murray and L. B. Confalonieri, eds., *Receptive Ecumenism and the Call to Catholic Learning: Exploring a Way for Contemporary Ecumenism* (Oxford University Press, 2008).

On the Pastoral Provision for Anglicans, and their life now as ordained Catholic priests, see the fascinating study by D. P. Sullins, *Keeping the Vow: The Untold Story of Married Catholic Priests* (Oxford University Press, 2015).

Ecclesiology has seen an explosion of studies over the last fifty years. One of the most influential, which has long shaped my own thinking here and elsewhere, is John Zizioulas's landmark *Being as Communion* (St. Vladimir's Seminary Press, 1997). For those desirous of a broader sweep, since to study ecclesiology is to study it ecumenically or not at all, a good place to start would be the new and hefty collection, *Oxford Handbook of Ecclesiology*, ed. Paul Avis (Oxford University Press, 2018). Other books of note would include Matthew Levering's *Christ and the Catholic Priesthood: Ecclesial Hierarchy and the Pattern of the Trinity* (Hillenbrand Books, 2010). For a similar approach to these issues, but from an Orthodox perspective, see the fascinating new study of Ashley Purpura, *God, Hierarchy, and Power: Orthodox Theologies of Authority from Byzantium* (Fordham University Press, 2017). In addition, see any of the books by the recently deceased John Quinn on papal reform as well as Vatican I. Thomas A. Baima has authored a useful monograph, *What is a Parish? Legal, Canonical, Pastoral and Theological Perspectives* (Chicago: Hillenbrand/Liturgy Training Publications, 2011).

Freud and *Future of an Illusion*: It is, I suppose, the unhappy fate of great men that they are invariably and widely subject to distortion by people too lazy to read them in the originals and then write about them accurately. Freud is especially prone to such shoddy treatment. If one cannot read him in the German original, then the Strachey *Standard Edition* is usually best, though for *Future of an Illusion* I would argue for the superiority of the G. C. Richter translation edited by Todd Dufresene and published by Broadview in 2012. For the best treatment of the analytic tradition and questions of God, see the Argentinian-American physician and psychoanalyst, Ana-María Rizzuto, who was raised Roman Catholic and taught in Catholic parishes in Argentina before coming to the US to finish medical and analytic training. Her groundbreaking 1979 book *The Birth of the Living God* (University of Chicago Press) was and remains the first major and successful attempt to move past Freud and, drawing in particular on Winnicott, and through extensive and detailed case studies of patients, to show that "God" is a concept and category the mind uses to understand the world — a "transitional object" even among children raised in "atheist" households. She remained very respectful of Freud even in her 1998 book, *Why Did Freud Reject God?: A Psychodynamic Interpretation*. Rizzuto's work is finally getting some of the sustained engagement it deserves in *Ana-María Rizzuto and the Psychoanalysis of Religion: The Road to the Living God*, M.J. Reineke and D.M. Goodman, eds. (2017).

The most important analyst writing today remains to my mind Adam Phillips, whose re-appropriation of Freud has greatly influenced my own. As I have noted in several places elsewhere, there is a considerable, though clearly unintentional, overlap between Phillips and the Christian tradition of apophaticism as seen, e.g., in Evagrius (and also in Pseudo-Dionysius, on whom, in this connection, see David Henderson, *Apophatic Elements in the Theory and Practice of Psychoanalysis: Pseudo-Dionysius and C.G. Jung* [Routledge, 2014]). See any number of Phillips's many titles, including *Unforbidden Pleasures: Rethinking Authority, Power, and Vitality* (2016); *On Kindness* (2010, with Barbara Taylor); *Missing Out: In Praise of the Unlived Life* (2013); *On Balance* (2011); *Side Effects* (2007); *The Beast in the Nursery: On Curiosity and Other Appetites* (1999); and *Terrors and Experts* (1997). There is a great deal of fresh, invigorating material here ripe for "despoiling" by Christians so inclined.

For other attempts to bring theology and psychoanalysis together, see Marcus Pound, *Theology, Psychoanalysis and Trauma* (2007), which has the merit of (almost) making Lacan's thought intelligible. The English psychoanalyst Nina Coltart's (d. 1997) charming and very delightful book, *Slouching towards Bethlehem and Further Psychoanalytic Explorations* (1992) is very much recommended for any number of insights, clinical and spiritual. She came out of Anglican Christianity to become Buddhist, but remained very open to and respectful of expressions of faith in herself and her patients. Stateside, Stanley A. Leavy (*In the*

Image of God: A Psychoanalyst's View) and Erich Fromm both deserve continued consideration, including the latter's most famous work *Escape from Freedom* (1941), as well as his *Beyond the Chains of Illusion: My Encounter with Marx and Freud* (1962); and most notably here, *Psychoanalysis and Religion* (1959). One very interesting and little known figure is W. W. Meissner, a Jesuit psychiatrist and analyst who died in 2010. See, e.g., his *Psychoanalysis and Religious Experience* (1986); *Life and Faith: Psychological Perspectives on Religious Experience* (1987); and *Ignatius of Loyola: the Psychology of a Saint* (1994).

Chapter 1: Toward a Future without Illusions

CHARLES TAYLOR IS ONE OF THE MOST IMPORTANT PHI-losophers alive today. In addition to his work on the social imaginary, see also his *Sources of the Self: the Making of Modern Identity* (Harvard University Press, 1992) and his 2007 tome, *A Secular Age* (Harvard). For a study on the imaginary of the Roman Empire, see Clifford Ando, *Roman Social Imaginaries: Language and Thought in the Context of Empire* (University of Toronto Press, 2012).

For a book that treats the themes of social imaginaries and much else in the work of Ricoeur and Castoriadis, see Suzi Adams, ed., *Ricoeur and Castoriadis in Discussion: On Human Creation, Historical Novelty, and the Social Imaginary* (Rowman and Littlefield, 2017).

For more on Joseph de Maistre, see Richard Lebrun and Carolina Armenteros, *Joseph de Maistre and his European Readers* (Brill, 2011). See also Armenteros's volume, *The French Idea of History: Joseph De Maistre and His Heirs, 1794–1854* (Cornell, 2011).

For the intersection of historiography and trauma psychoanalytically understood, Vamik Volkan remains indispensable. In addition to *Bloodlines*, see also his 2006 book *Killing in the Name of Identity: A Study of Bloody Conflicts*. There and elsewhere he has shown how many people reconstruct ethnic and national histories (and also, I would add, some Christian histories) to reflect either "chosen trauma" or "chosen glory."

Two other important scholars are doing work in similar veins. See Jeffrey Prager of UCLA, especially his *Presenting the Past: Psychoanalysis and the Sociology of Misremembering* (Harvard University

Press, 1998). Additionally, David Levine of the University of Colorado has written a number of books here, including *Psychoanalysis, Society, and the Inner World: Embedded Meaning in Politics and Social Conflict* (2017), which suggestively applies analytic insights (especially those of Winnicott and the object relations school) to the age of "fake news," rising nationalism, and identity politics. An early, and still controversial, work is Donald P. Spence, *Narrative Truth and Historical Truth: Meaning and Interpretation in Psychoanalysis* (W. W. Norton, 1982), which is useful in trying to understand contemporary forms of propaganda.

Chapter 2: Reforming Parish Councils

FOR HISTORY OF THE DIOCESE OF HURON SEE MARK RICHardson, *A Light in the Forest: 150 Years of The Diocese of Huron* (2008). For a wider history of Canadian Anglicanism see Alan L. Hayes, *Anglicans in Canada: Controversies and Identity in Historical Perspective* (University of Illinois Press, 2004). For a global overview of the Anglican Communion, see I. S. Markham et al., eds., *The Wiley-Blackwell Companion to the Anglican Communion* (2013).

For Anglican polity see House of Deputies, *Shared Governance: The Polity of the Episcopal Church* (Church Publishing, 2012). See especially the new and fascinating book by Ellen K. Wondra, *Questioning Authority: The Theology and Practice of Authority in the Episcopal Church and Anglican Communion* (Peter Lang, 2018).

For practical advice on parish councils, see Mary Ann Gubish, Susan Jenny, and Arlene McGannon, *Revisioning the Parish Pastoral Council: A Workbook* (Paulist Press, 2001).

Chapter 3: Returning to Regular Diocesan Synods

FOR MANY WORKS ON SYNODALITY AT THE DIOCESAN, regional, and patriarchal levels, see the extensive discussion and literature in my *Orthodoxy and the Roman Papacy.* Since its publication, a few new works have come along of some importance, including Norman Tanner, *The Church in Council: Conciliar Movements, Religious Practice and the Papacy from Nicaea to Vatican II* (IB Tauris, 2011).

For late medieval history of French and English synods, see the relevant chapters in *Canon Law, Religion, and Politics: Liber Amicorum Robert Somerville*, eds. Uta-Renate Blumenthal et al. (Catholic University of America Press, 2012). Most recently, see the 2018 document "Synodality in the Life and Mission of the Church," published by the International Theological Commission and available on the Vatican website.

For more on sovereignty, see Paul W. Kahn, *Political Theology: Four New Chapters on the Concept of Sovereignty* (Columbia University Press, 2011); and more generally, Jean Bethke Elshtain, *Sovereignty: God, State, and Self* (Basic, 2008).

The Jesuit theologian Francis Sullivan has written many useful works of relevance to much of this book. For the purposes of this chapter, see in particular his "Provincial Councils and the Choosing of Priests for Appointment as Bishops," *Theological Studies* 74 (2013).

Chapter 4: Reforming Episcopal Conferences

AGAIN, SEE THE EXTENSIVE LITERATURE REVIEWED AND analyzed in my *Orthodoxy and the Roman Papacy*.

On the Council of Serdica, Hamilton Hess has long remained the definitive authority in a volume he updated after a half-century of scholarship: *The Early Development of Canon Law and the Council of Serdica* (Oxford University Press, 2003). For more on Serdica, see also Christopher Stephens, *Canon Law and Episcopal Authority: The Canons of Antioch and Serdica* (Oxford, 2015).

Chapter 5: Married Priests and Bishops?

THE BEST BOOK TO LOOK WIDELY AND SERIOUSLY AT THE challenges of married priesthood from a variety of angles—historical, canonical, theological, ecumenical, and biographical—is my own, forthcoming from the University of Notre Dame Press: *Married Catholic Priests: A Primer*. With contributions from Eastern Catholics, Roman Catholics, Eastern Orthodox, and sometime Anglican clerics in Europe and North America, as well as Australia, it represents the fullest contribution to the literature to date.

The topic of married bishops has received, to date, almost no serious treatment in Anglophone theological literature. The one exception is the Greek Orthodox scholar P. I. Boumes, in a two-part article published in the *Greek Orthodox Theological Review* vol. 29 (1984) and volume 40 in 1995. He notes that some Orthodox mistakenly assume that married bishops are forbidden, whereas his work shows that they were gradually restricted canonically at and after the Quinisext Council (of Trullo) in reflection of current social mores, but that there are no canonical, still less scriptural or patristic, reasons to forbid married bishops. He argues that any local church that wished to revive this practice could do so, though it would be preferable for all churches to come to prior agreement.

In the twentieth century, there were two brief and aborted discussions about reviving married bishops, both in the same timeframe. The Orthodox semi-synod in Constantinople in 1923 did discuss it briefly; and during the same immediate postwar period, the Orthodox Churches in Ukraine toyed with the idea. On the former gathering, see Patrick Viscuso's book *A Quest for Reform of the Orthodox Church: The 1923 Pan-Orthodox Congress, An Analysis and Translation of Its Acts and Decisions* (Inter-Orthodox Press, 2007). On the latter, see the superb new book by Nicholas Denysenko, *The Orthodox Church in Ukraine: A Century of Separation* (Northern Illinois University Press, 2018).

For more of Claudia Rapp's scholarship on bishops, sexuality, and asceticism, especially in the antique Byzantine church, see "Desert, City, and Countryside in the Early Christian Imagination," *Church History and Religious Culture* 86 (2006): 93–112. Here she notes an early example of an "imaginary" at work as the desert played on the Christian mind as the place where one could be free of all attachments such as marriage and sexuality in search of some supposedly purified celibate ideal. For a longer, fuller study of many of these themes, see her *Holy Bishops in Late Antiquity: The Nature of Christian Leadership in an Age of Transition* (University of California Press, 2013).

For additional studies on the history and changes in celibacy in the Latin priesthood, see, inter alia, E. C. Cage, *Unnatural Frenchmen: The Politics of Priestly Celibacy and Marriage, 1720–1815* (University of Virginia Press, 2015); Helen Parish, *Clerical Celibacy in the West*

1100–1700 (Routledge, 2010); Michael Frassetto, *Medieval Purity and Piety: Essays on Medieval Clerical Celibacy and Religious Reform* (Routledge, 1998); and most recently, Maroula Perisanidi, *Clerical Continence in Twelfth-Century England and Byzantium: Property, Family, and Purity* (Routledge, 2018).

ACKNOWLEDGMENTS

I AM GRATEFUL TO MANY PEOPLE FOR THEIR input at various stages, starting with my dear friend, the priest Jason Charron, pastor of Holy Trinity Ukrainian Catholic Church in Carnegie, PA. He read through the entire draft and gave extremely detailed and very helpful feedback, not sparing my blushes in making several serious criticisms in places that only made this book stronger. The anonymous reviewers for Angelico Press, capably directed by John Riess of the press, also made very useful suggestions for revisions, and I thank them and him for this helpful feedback graciously conveyed. I also thank Michael Martin for his superlative copy-editing, and his excellent assistance on many points not just of style but also of substance.

My Orthodox friends, the scholars and priests Michael Plekon and William Mills, were extremely encouraging. Their support of this project was invaluable.

My friend Greg Erlandson, formerly of *Our Sunday Visitor* and now president of Catholic News Service, offered very helpful insights into the world of Catholic publishing and more generally American intra-Catholic politics.

My uncle by marriage, Philip Sandstrom, is a longstanding priest of the Archdiocese of New York, ordained by Cardinal Spellman in 1962 before undertaking doctoral studies in Paris and ministering in Belgium for decades now. His international pastoral perspective was very helpful and gave me several important insights as I was writing.

I thank the University of Saint Francis — where it has been my delight to teach for nearly a dozen years now — for the gift of a sabbatical during which this book was written.

It is — as I learned many years ago from Stanley Hauerwas — one of the greatest undeserved gifts of the academic life that one's students are often one's best teachers. Thus it is that I thank Mark Robbins, who wrote his MA thesis with me at USF nearly a decade ago now, and has become a most perceptive and discerning critic as well as friend. He and his lovely wife Jan read through the entire manuscript and both offered very detailed and enormously helpful feedback based on their long and very revealing experience in Latin parish governance and Roman Catholic schools.

I am thankful to the Chicago Psychoanalytic Institute for the provision of a year-long fellowship, which has helped clarify some of my thinking about Freud and psychoanalysis. For the practice of the same, I am profoundly grateful for the life-changing labors of the late Dr. Louise Carignan of Ottawa and Dr. Mary Landy of Indianapolis. I also thank the Cincinnati Psychoanalytic Institute, whose library was so generously made available to me for early research.

Finally, I thank Annemarie and our four splendid children, Ephraim, Aidan, Anastasia, and Helena, "who rise up and call her blessed" (Prov. 31:28), as do I.

INDEX

ABOUT THE AUTHOR

ADAM A. J. DEVILLE is an associate professor in the theology department and director of humanities at the University of Saint Francis in Ft. Wayne, IN; and editor-in-chief of *Logos: A Journal of Eastern Christian Studies.*

Made in the USA
San Bernardino, CA
14 March 2019